THE GREAT COLLAPSE

WALDMAN

Public Service Publishing Co.
NEW YORK

THE GREAT COLLAPSE

HIGHER FARES OR PUBLIC OWNERSHIP

BY

LOUIS WALDMAN

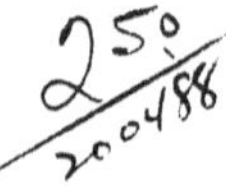
250
200488

ARTES
SCIENTIA
VERITAS
LIBRARY OF THE
UNIVERSITY OF MICHIGAN
TUEBOR
CIRCUMSPICE
TRANSPORTATION
LIBRARY

THE GREAT COLLAPSE

Higher Fares
OR
Public Ownership

BY

LOUIS WALDMAN

Introduction by

SCOTT NEARING

BONI AND LIVERIGHT

PUBLISHERS NEW YORK

Printed in the United States of America

To

My Brother, Morris Waldman

PREFACE

THE general chaotic condition of our transportation facilities and the threatened and accomplished bankruptcies have convinced the writer of the supreme need for a popular explanation of the whole problem of private ownership and management of public utilities. The persistent campaign of the traction trust for an increase in fares, not only in New York but in almost every large city in the country, has been calculated to convey the impression that the railroad companies are great public benefactors imposed upon by an ungrateful public.

A concerted effort is being made, in many cases successfully, to hold up the public for more loot. In this city, although some ground has already been lost by the extra charge for transfers, the people are still holding out against further encroachment by the corporations.

To strengthen the hand of the people in their fight, to equip them with arguments, facts and general knowledge of the situation, is the purpose of this book.

Although written with special reference to New York it is nevertheless of general interest because the essential features of the railroad problem in this city are the same as those in most of the cities in the country. Moreover, the methods the corporations pursue, the modes of business organization, the general laws of development of the traction system in this city partake of the general character of modern large industry. The suggestions for legislative relief here made are, with slight variations, applicable to the national railroads as well as to most of the other socially necessary industries.

Having in mind the difficulties the average person has in understanding technical business terms, such as amortization, common stock, preferred stock, bonds, corporations, leases, operating agreements and holding companies, it has been deemed advisable to devote the first few chapters to an explanation of the meaning of these terms and of the modern instruments of business organization. Once the reader has secured a clear knowledge of these, he will have no difficulty in following the facts related in the subsequent chapters.

This book will have achieved its purpose if it succeeds in revealing the obscure operations of the traction trust and throws some light on the perplexing problems which are pressing hard for immediate solution.

Armed with the knowledge of the methods the capitalists employ, the reader will be able to judge for himself whether the claims made by the defenders of the present order of private ownership of social needs are correct, or whether the claims of its assailants, the proponents of the new system, the system of social ownership and democratic management of industry, are correct.

The traction problem in New York presents amazing incongruities. Busy trains, crowded cars, comparatively short trips, and yet the companies complain and show figures proving that they cannot successfully operate on a five cent fare! The following study exposes their deceptive and vicious practices and shows their "proof" fallacious. It clearly demonstrates the financial possibilities of operating the lines successfully on even less than a five cent fare.

The circumstances of the recent bankruptcies are given at the very outset, in order to enable the reader to see for himself the extent to which the lords of high finance are permitted to go under their own capitalist-made laws to cajole the public into doing their bidding.

Many public documents and official reports have been issued, containing all the facts of the case, but owing to the bulk and dry nature of these reports the facts have escaped the notice of the public. The story stating the plain facts in plain language has not yet been written. As far as the writer knows this is the first attempt.

While it is undoubtedly true that private ownership and management of public utilities is the source of the existing inconveniences, high rates, and general chaos, it is not sufficiently convincing merely to say so; such conclusion must be backed by showing specifically where this private ownership is responsible for these evils.

And even this is not sufficient. It is necessary to point the way out of the difficulties. General proposals, such as "public ownership is the remedy," may have been well enough when it was confined to the domain of propaganda, but not when it enters the realm of practical legislation. The time has arrived when it is essential that we get a clear idea of what our proposals really mean.

Only by educating people to the real meaning of public ownership can there be created an enlightened public opinion to resist the enactment of sham reform measures, parading under the popular name of public ownership. The various phases of public ownership are discussed in the last few chapters. It should be borne in mind, however, that the suggestions there made are not offered as ultimate solutions, but as steps to secure immediate relief while the present system of private ownership still predominates.

In publishing this little volume, the writer is indebted to Miss Sylvia Miller and Gertrude Weil Klein for their kind assistance in preparing the manuscript, and to his friend William Morris Feigenbaum for his kind assistance and valuable suggestions.

L. W.

INTRODUCTION

THE economic history of the United States is wonderfully enriched by the records of the street-railway organization. Capitalism, at its best and at its worst, is mirrored in the transactions that have turned hundreds of millions in city franchise values over to a clique of private exploiters, who have made it a point to use the advantage of their monopolistic position to fill their own pockets. Through the whole story, there is no known instance where the street railways, under private management, have been operated for the purpose of furnishing transportation. Instead, transportation was furnished as a means of making money. Profit—not service—is the aim of this, as it is the aim of every other part of the capitalistic organization of our economic life.

The tale is simple, consecutive and dramatic. The capitalists came; they saw; they appropriated. Thereafter they reaped millions in profits.

As the cities grew, and it became impossible for people to walk or drive to their work, their trade or their pleasure, a need arose for some means of quick, dependable, cheap transportation. The streets were there—graded and paved.

Plainly, those who could get the right to the use of these streets, for the transportation purposes, had a source of immense income value.

Promoters recognized the value of these franchises. Office-holders, as the trustees of the public rights had it in their power to dispose of them—almost as they chose, until the immensity of the issues at stake were called to public attention. The result was easily foreseen. The politicians sold, the financiers bought. There ensued that disgraceful period of corruption, during the forty years following the Civil War, that has made the municipal government of the United States a byword among students of public affairs in all parts of the world.

The financiers, once in possession of the franchises, manipulated, leased, rented, consolidated, merged, combined. Watered stocks flooded the markets. Preposterous contracts were made. Millions in social values were pocketed by men who never turned a hand to render a public service. These financial transactions, and these contracts form the basis for the demands that the street-railway interests are at present making upon the American public.

For years the people have been paying huge

returns on stolen, inflated values. Now costs are rising. It is becoming difficult or impossible for the companies to live up to the robber agreements planned and executed during the past fifty years. So the people are asked to pay again.

No one has stated that passengers cannot be carried at the present rate of fare. The Cleveland experiment has amply proved the contrary. It is contended that at the present rate of fare, vested interests in stolen property cannot be compensated at the rates agreed upon among the original thieves.

The following pages tell this story for New York, a story that every New Yorker must know if he expects to deal intelligently with the traction controversy during the next few months. The history of New York traction is typical—therefore it is doubly important. It is a symptom—pointing, inexorably to the disease.

The story of the street-railway debauchery, told here for New York alone, has been repeated with sickening uniformity in one American city after another. The amounts involved in New York are larger. The principle everywhere is the same.

The experience which the people of New York

and other American cities have had with their street railways is broad enough and bitter enough to convince even the most skeptical that the only safe place for public property is in public hands. Private ownership of public utilities means private profits from public sources. The people must own if they are to rule.

SCOTT NEARING.

CONTENTS

CHAPTER I

THE COLLAPSE

THE Brooklyn Rapid Transit System officially collapsed on December 31, 1918. From the standpoint of service there had been nothing to collapse. Its greatest efforts had been in the direction of extracting nickels from the people's pockets to the extent of almost $30,000,000 annually.

To the traveling public the B. R. T. has become a veritable torture. It is a common jest that the B. R. T. is the railroad that makes walking a pleasure. It is as safe to travel on a B. R. T. train as it is to be on a ship sailing in mined waters. Of late, accidents on this system have been a common occurrence.

The bankruptcy of this company, therefore, will not be mourned by many. The people see in it a hope for relief. Perhaps, at last, public officials will bestir themselves to solve the problem.

"Judge Julius M. Mayer of the United States District Court," said Timothy S. Williams, president of the B. R. T., on January 1, 1919, "to-day made an order appointing ex-Secretary of War

Lindley M. Garrison receiver of the Brooklyn Rapid Transit Railroad Company, the New York Municipal Railroad Corporation, and the New York Consolidated Railroad Corporation, these two being subsidiaries of the Brooklyn Rapid Transit Company. The order was made upon the application of the Westinghouse Electric Manufacturing Company, a creditor, for material furnished. *The companies did not oppose the action, for they felt that they would be subserved by a temporary receivership.**

"The immediate requirements were meeting, January 1st, obligations for about $2,000,000, and *this could have been obtained,** but to complete the construction and equipment work now under contract and to provide for additional expenditures for similar purposes during the coming year, will require the raising of many millions more, and the general situation affecting street railroads, with their stationary fares and rising costs, had injured their credit and made impossible up to the present time provision for the investment of fresh capital."

Col. Williams goes on to state that "the effort on the part of the company to restore rates of

* Italics are mine.

fares authorized by their franchises or to get the right to charge fares sufficient to meet the costs of service, has thus far failed."

Three things are clear from this statement.

First—The company, for the B. R. T. is really only one company, contends that a five-cent fare, which it had agreed to charge, is no longer "sufficient to meet the costs of service," and that all its effort "to get the right to charge" a seven-cent fare "has thus far failed."

Second—That the company did not have to go into bankruptcy at this time. It could have met its obligations to the Westinghouse Electric Manufacturing Company, but chose this course because of its apparent inability to raise money for probable needs in the future. It "felt" that its interest "would be subserved by a temporary receivership."

Third—That President Williams did not oppose the application of the creditor company. On the contrary, he joined in the petition of the plaintiff company that the Federal Court take over the property for the protection of the creditors, bondholders and stockholders.

Professor Gerstenberg of New York University says that a receiver is supposed to be "an *impartial person** appointed by an equity court to hold and administer any property which is the subject of litigation."†

Travis H. Whitney, a former Public Service Commissioner, was quoted in the New York *Times* of January 1, 1919 as having said that Mr. Garrison was named receiver at the suggestion of George D. Yoemans, counsel of the B. R. T. Moreover, only one week prior to his appointment, Mr. Garrison was selected by the company as its representative on an arbitration committee to decide whether the large awards likely to grow out of the terrible Malbone Street accident should be charged against operating expenses.

Obviously Mr. Garrison does not exactly meet the test of Professor Gerstenberg's definition. He is an acknowledged friend of the Brooklyn Rapid Transit Company.

All circumstances seem to indicate that this receivership was staged for the benefit of a public unwilling to grant increased fares to the traction companies of the city.

On the 2nd day of January, 1919, taking advantage of the excitement caused by the collapse

---

* Italics are mine.

† Modern Business, page 164.

of the Brooklyn Rapid Transit System, Theodore P. Shonts, president of the Interborough Rapid Transit Company, sent a letter to the Public Service Commission and the Board of Estimate and Apportionment renewing his former application for permission to charge higher fares. He did better than his sister companies, requesting an eight-cent fare for his system. It was, of course, the psychological moment to insist that "the city can gain nothing by starving the Interborough into bankruptcy."*

The New York Railways Company, a street surface railway corporation, holding the club of bankruptcy over a frightened public, came with a like request. In a word, all the important traction systems of New York received an irresistable impetus in their demand for increased fares. A systematic campaign has been launched in the press. The statements of the companies, interspersed with spicy and friendly journalistic arguments, are published on the front pages.†

The reactionary section of the press, true to its mission, has taken up the fight on behalf of the

* N. Y. *Times*, January 1st, 1919.

† Since this chapter was written, the New York Railways Company has been placed in the hands of a receiver, Mr. Job E. Hedges.

corporations with great zeal. It employs the usual tactics of appealing to the people's good nature and extreme sense of fairness. It understands how the plain people abhor driving anyone to ruin. Thus, the New York *Times* of January 3, 1919, in an editorial entitled "*The City's Responsibility*," said:

"The remedy of increased fares which has averted bankruptcies in so many other cities is the one indicated here."

In a long editorial protesting innocence of any unsound financial dealings on the part of the companies, and bewailing the "loss and ruin to the unfortunate investors," the New York *Sun* of January 3, 1919, said:

"Now there is only one way out of affording relief to the companies. It is to convert the average loss on every passenger carried into an average gain. The companies have no way of making money save out of passenger fares. The present fare nets the loss from which the companies are perishing. Obviously the fare must be raised. Nothing seems to afford an alternative to this course."

Fortunately, the concerted effort of the press creates no impression on the people. The appeals seem to fall on deaf ears. There is little sympathy for the companies.

The Brooklyn Rapid Transit Company trains run as usual, if not with greater regularity. There is no difference as far as the public is concerned whether the company is technically solvent or not.

The old conception of bankruptcy is obsolete. It has changed with the introduction of new methods in business organization. The railroads are no longer in the hands of individual proprietors. They are now carried on by corporations.

When the individual proprietor was declared bankrupt he personally suffered. There was a human touch in his plight. Socially it was a calamity to him. The debts he could not pay and which drove him to bankruptcy he usually owed to people he knew. They were members of the same church, of the same club, of the same community with him. They thought highly of him and he cherished their good will. He who had been a reputable citizen in the community now would be a marked man. Economically he was even more to be pitied. It meant his complete ruin. He would become absolutely helpless. His entire wealth, including his personal property, could be taken from him to discharge his obligations. It may have meant unmitigated poverty for himself and his family. Such possibilities evoked sympathy and fear.

The Brooklyn Rapid Transit bankruptcy or, for that matter, most corporation bankruptcies, are "business" affairs. There is no human element. The history of the traction system in New York City is the history of bankruptcies and reorganizations. For the press to continue to play the chord of sympathy is useless.

Public utility corporations in New York seem indeed to thrive on bankruptcies. After each failure, instead of reorganizing the business on a sound basis, eliminating the causes that led to the insolvency, just the reverse has been done. Not only have the poisons that ate the system's financial tissues, bringing it to ruin, been retained, but more of them were added. They multiplied weakness upon weakness with every reorganization. Every attempt on the part of government commissions to place the companies upon a solid footing has been fought bitterly. The investors, bankers and trust companies, the real controllers of the transit systems, seem to feed on the weaknesses of corporations, as vultures feed and grow fat on corpses.

The New York Railways Company, which so loudly protests its innocence of corporate wrong-doing, is a classic example of corporation brazenness. This corporation is erected upon the ruins of the Metropolitan Street Railway Company. In 1911, when the organizers of the new corporation applied to the Public Service Commission, then in its infancy, for permission to issue new securities, the latter, upon a careful examination of the properties and a study of its outstanding debts, declined to grant the application. The Commission claimed that the securities the company sought to issue would be far above the physical value of the property; that if the securities as proposed by the companies were issued the system would be based on a false foundation and would lead either to excessive charges in the way of fares or to bankruptcy. The companies, instead of disproving the contentions of the Commission, turned to the courts for assistance. The courts held that the Commission had no right to look into the securities issued by a reorganized company if the issue did not exceed the aggregate debts of the constituent companies.

The New York Railways Company was quite willing to avail itself of this decision to prevent the Public Service Commission from protecting "poor unfortunate investors," as well as the great mass of fare-payers from being robbed.

One item for which the company issued securities was $4,740,000 to cover "Initial payments for franchises" and "Interest on franchise security deposits," which was never spent on these items; at least, such an amount was never spent. The company does not disclose who got this money. Under the head of "Organization and Finance," the company issued securities to cover $8,149,580. The items making up this huge sum consist of such well deserved and indispensable expense as "Payments to underwriting syndicates,—$2,400,000." The results of the issue of such securities will be shown in detail in a later chapter.

The Commission refused to give its consent to this gross imposition upon the public pocketbook. It was later directed by the court to give its approval to the company's application, and it did.

The companies won. They did not win by proving the charges of over-capitalization made by the Public Service Commission to have been false. They did not win by proving that for every dollar of security issued there existed its equivalent in property. They fought the Commission on a legal technicality.

The court's decision has carried with it millions of dollars to the promoters and bankers, excessive fares, poor service to the public, and probably low wages to the railway employees.

The outstanding fact is that these companies now pleading financial embarrassment, threatening bankruptcy, appealing to our sympathies in their efforts to secure permission to charge higher fares, deliberately chose to avail themselves of a legal technicality when it suited their purpose to do so. They reorganized the bankrupt business in a manner clearly carrying within itself the germs of future bankruptcy. It was not done out of ignorance; it was done to make money. It paid to cast sound business principles to the wind and choose the path of speculation.

The Commission argued not only in the New York Railways Company case, but also in the case of the Third Avenue Railway Company, that the companies could not succeed, for they were loading the business more than the traffic could bear. The organizers responded: "You have no legal right to say that." They did not claim: "You are not correct in your contention."

And now, with the echoes of the Commission's warning still ringing in our ears, these corporations impudently use the club of bankruptcy over the public to exact permission to charge higher fares. The impudence of the corporations is measured only by the tolerance of the public.

Chapter II

THE CORPORATION

AS INSTRUMENT OF BUSINESS ORGANIZATION AND CONCEALER OF PROFITS

A corporation is an excellent instrument for concealing the true earnings of capital. The average man is not familiar with the intricacies of modern business organization. He loses himself in the maze of technical words. Common stock, preferred stock, cumulative bonds, adjustment bonds, are all so many mysteries to him. And it is precisely here where the corporations prevail over the public.

A financial statement issued by a traction company, for example, will show conclusively that it is losing money or that it is just "breaking even." The public wonders how such a thing is possible in a city where the cars are nearly always filled to capacity, and in busy hours jammed beyond human endurance. But figures are figures; figures do not lie, although, it is said, liars do figure.

The proof is "conclusive," yet unbelievable. Out of the mist of doubt arise vague and indefinite ideas. In due time, by a constant presentation of the "proof," the human mind begins to question.

After all, why should these companies be singled out for ill treatment? Why victimize them? Why should the investors be compelled to lose money on the public? Everybody is compensated for services rendered—why not the railroad companies? Transportation is most essential; and if the figures show, and they do show, that a five-cent fare does not cover expenses, then there is nothing left to do but to raise the fares. Such is the reasoning of the average person. The question of fair play does enter into his calculations.

The conservative citizen sees in this situation more than that. He sees in it a justification for his preconceived prejudice against collective ownership of industry generally and municipal ownership of railroads in particular. Had the city owned the transit system, he reasons, we would have had a 7 or 8 cent fare long ago. In fact, the companies in their campaign literature for higher fares make precisely this argument. He is sure that with a five-cent fare the city would either go bankrupt, or burden the taxpayers with the losses. In either case, it would be worse than what we now have, and he is happy there is no municipal ownership. Moreover, he is convinced, now more than ever, that there never should be municipal ownership.

These conclusions are logical deductions based on information furnished by the companies. The information is calculated to lead to just such conclusions. Those who furnish it know what they are doing.

Nothing, however, could be further from the truth than these conclusions. *The cold facts are that the roads are earning profits, big profits, even now under a five-cent fare, notwithstanding the financial statements of the companies to the contrary.* The trouble is that the figures in these financial reports are not properly examined. The *actual* is not separated from the *alleged* expense. Interest on bonds to this or that bank, dividends on preferred stock for this or that company, rentals on leases, amortization of bonds representing no actual investment in the business, are all thrown into expenses, although in reality they are pure profit.

These "expenses," which run into tens of millions of dollars annually, amount to almost half of the total expense as shown in the Annual Report of the Interborough Rapid Transit Company for the year ended June 30, 1918. The same financial condition is true of the other transit companies in the city. Yet these "expenses" represent nothing but fat profits.

In its early days capitalism was simple enough. The game was an open one. Everybody comprehended its rules. Shrewd lawyers were not needed at every step. Expert brokers were useless. When individual proprietorships and simple partnerships prevailed it was easy to calculate the profits earned.

If a business with an investment of $10,000 at the end of the fiscal year, having paid and deducted all expenses, had $700 left, it was clear to all that a 7 per cent. profit had been earned; if $1,400 were left, a 14 per cent. profit. There was no difficulty in finding out whether the business paid.

Not so with a corporation. Ten thousand dollars' actual investment in a corporation may have had issued against it $10,000 worth of common stock, $10,000 of preferred stock and $20,000 worth of bonds. Whatever profits a corporation earns must be apportioned to the bondholders first, the preferred stockholders next and, if there is any money left, to the holders of common stock. If the corporation in question at the end of a fiscal year, with expenses deducted, finds $1,400 made, and if the interest on the bonds, which are generally fixed, happens to be 7 per cent., the $1,400 would be used to pay interest to the bondholders. The stockholders of both classes would receive nothing. No dividends to anybody, yet a 14 per cent. profit would have been made on the money invested.

How easy it would be for the corporations to plead poverty before a gullible public! They could show black on white that they were operating at a loss.

The instance here cited is by no means far-fetched or overstated; on the contrary, it is the corporation method of concealing profits in its simplest and most innocent form. In practice the manipulation is far more subtle. Losses are frequently shown on financial reports when, in fact, profits are earned on the money invested.

Properly to understand the claims of our public utility corporations and to know how much we are gouged, it will be necessary to make a simple and succinct statement of the meaning of the modern instrument of business organization, the corporation. It will also be essential to unravel the hopeless and confusing situation of leases, partial control, full control, operating agreements and holding companies. The knots in our railroad system will be untied so that the length of the rope may be seen by all.

It is difficult to define a corporation to include all elements. "According to contemporary practice, a corporation is an association of natural persons, or of other legally constituted persons (other companies), authorized by law to act as a unit, under a corporate name, for the accomplishment of certain definite and prescribed purposes. . . . It is a 'person' constituted by a law, separate and distinct from its stockholders, and, in a certain sense, is a citizen."*

A corporation is an association of individuals recognized by law as an entity. It has an existence of its own; it bears its own name, builds its own reputation, leads its own life; it is a "person," a creature of the law; it can become insolvent, it can die, it can become revived; it can do many questionable things without in the least hurting or embarrassing those respectable members of the community who constitute it.

* W. Allen, Modern Business Corporation, p. 1.

The value of the property of a corporation is reprepsented by what is known as stock. It is divided into shares, usually, of one hundred dollars each. A share is a certificate showing ownership in the corporation. A holder of a one hundred dollar share does not own one hundred dollars' worth of property in the business. He does own one hundred dollars' worth of control in the corporation. A citizen of the United States does not, by virtue of his citizenship, own any part of the United States, but does own a right in the government of the country. A stockholder, likewise, owns a right in the government of the corporation which owns the property.

Stock is generally divided into two classes, preferred and common. That class of stock earning dividends before any other, having priority in the assets of the corporation in case of failure, is called preferred stock. The stock that lays last claim on the assets in case of failure and earns dividends after all other claims have been satisfied, including the payment of dividends on preferred stock, is called common stock.

The control of the corporation is usually in the reverse order. The common stock gets first control; preferred stock next, and under certain contingencies, bondholders may step in.

A corporation may issue bonds to obtain finances. They are usually secured by a mortgage on the property. Railroad corporations in this state must obtain permission from the Public Service Commission before issuing bonds.

A bond is a certificate of indebtedness bearing a fixed and guaranteed interest which must be paid periodically. In case of inability to pay such interest, the court, upon the application of the bondholders, declares the corporation insolvent, takes the management away from the stockholders and places the business in the hands of a receiver to run it in the interest of the bondholders.

The bondholders stand no risk. Their earnings are definite. The lords of high finance refuse to take chances. They will let the small fry run the business, pride themselves on owning things, give an opportunity to professors to write books attempting to disprove the theory of concentration of wealth—they will permit all this, but they will never allow anything to interfere with their sapping the vitality of industry by drawing usurious interest, nor will they permit industry to escape their control. Most of the railroad companies are financed by bond issues.

The courts describe corporations as being "soulless." A glance at the history of our public utility corporations will convince one that the courts are right.

The law, creating a new substance in a corporation, apes nature. Chemical substances are generally distinct from their elements. Water is not a sum of hydrogen and oxygen, it is their product. It is not a gas but a liquid. A corporation, likewise, is not the sum of so many individuals, but a product of them. Three men A, B and C form a partnership, the result is a business of A + B + C. Each partner is responsible for the entire firm. If A is a prince and B and C are paupers, A will be held responsible for the business transactions entered into by B and C on behalf of the partnerships. The credit and value of the firm is the sum of the three partners. Each partner stakes his personal reputation and fortune in the business.

If, however, A, B and C form a corporation, the result is a business of A B C, a new creature. Each member risks an amount equal to the par value of the stock he owns, beyond which the creditors cannot reach him. The business is carried on by a Board of Directors elected by the stockholders.

Those who oppose socialism because it would destroy "individual initiative" and "incentive" to personal effort, thereby destroying the "foundation of modern society," must revise their views. The corporation, the chosen instrument of capitalism, has already destroyed individual initiative and incentive to personal effort. A corporation is impersonal; it is an institution, a collectivity, legally possesing some attributes of a natural person carrying on its business activities through *hired brains*. Where personal service is of the essence a corporation cannot function. Thus, the law in New York forbids dentists, physicians and lawyers to carry on business as a corporate body.

A corporation is essentially a modern instrument of business organization. Prior to 1776 only two business corporations had been chartered in this country.

The first quarter of the nineteenth century was the beginning of the present industrial system.

Capitalism was in its youth. It was vigorous, enterprising, almost feverish in its growth. Then corporations were given the greatest stimulus. Many of the states, by enacting favorable statutes, facilitated the organization of corporations. With practically no legal check, the corporation in its adolescent stages indulged in unspeakable vices. It resorted to every trick known to the business charlatan.

"It was asserted that a small clique of Boston capitalists by improper methods perpetuated voting control of those corporations in which they owned a comparatively small amount of stock. They induced stockholders to sign proxies in their favor when they signed their dividend receipts. They also held annual meetings, in small rooms, to which but a fraction of the shareholders could get access, and called meetings of several companies at different places for the same day and hour, in order to divide the oposition of independent men who owned stock in a number of companies. Less than a score of Boston capitalists were said thus to dictate the fortunes of most of the great manufacturing corporations of the State, and one man was cited who was director of 23 companies and president of all. The same coterie owned a Massachusetts Life-Insurance Company, which, with a capital of $500,000, controlled nearly 10 times that amount of investment funds. Having forced factories by mismanagement to accept loans by this company, they either foreclosed or used every power to depress stock for their own benefit. The other spoil of this control was high-salaried officers and exhorbitant agents' commissions."*

A similar story of early abuses might be told with equal truth of New York traction companies. Many evil practices exist even now, but such as are pictured above are too crude for the modern financiers. They can stifle opposition and obtain control in a more "respectable" and "legal" way. The modern is the scientific method of robbery.

The fact that the corporation can be used as an instrument for corruption did not deter industry from selecting it as the most logical and adaptable instrument of business organization. Between individual proprietorships, partnerships and corporations there was a fierce struggle for existence, and the corporations won. Almost three-

* History of Manufacturers, 1607-1860, p. 460; quoted in Modern Business, C. W. Gerstenberg, p. 9.

quarters of the wage earners of this land are employed in corporate industry. The basic industries of the country are almost all in the hands of corporations.

What is the real reason for the conquest of the corporation over the individual proprietorship? What is the efficient cause, as it were, for the selection of the corporate mode of business organization? Why do business men deliberately choose this instrument as against all others? While undoubtedly the vicious element in the business world will at times prefer the corporate method because of the opportunities it offers for corrupt practices, the vast majority of business men do it purely because of its superiority over all other modes of organization. Any agency can be abused and its purposes perverted.

Modern industry, especially the railroad business, required three indispensable elements: permanency, large size and limitation of risk. The corporate method assures all these.

Permanency is essential in the railroad business. It would be difficult to confer a franchise right upon an individual or partnership, because the enterprise would be dependent upon the skill or lack of skill, ability or inability, whims, fancies, and the life of human beings. Upon the death of an owner or a partner in whom, principally, trust and reliance was placed, the business may descend by inheritance or otherwise to individuals incompetent and untrustworthy. Evidently, such possibilities and unstable conditions are impossible in a business where permanent fixtures are built at great expense and put to stay. The initial expense of a railroad is very large and is growing larger daily. A railroad cannot be moved about, or otherwise subjected to disturbances. The life of the business cannot be measured by and should not depend upon the life of a human being.

A corporation, on the other hand, is not subject to the whims and fancies of stockholders. It is run in accordance with certain prescribed laws. The death of an investor does not in the least affect the progress or life of the corporation. If a stockholder cannot agree with the rest of the investors the corporation is not dissolved, he simply sells his shares to someone else. The business does not suffer thereby. Order, permanency, are the law of the modern business world.

Of course, under certain circumstances, a corporation, too, can be dissolved; but its dissolution is a rare thing. It is accomplished either when it violates the purpose for which it was organized, and the state finds it necessary to interfere, or, on the decision of two-thirds of its stockholders.

This is the age of big business. Even those who rail against "monopolies" and "trusts" concede that. President Wilson, in a masterly brief for the middle class, said: "I am for big business, but against monopoly."* Any instrument of business organization that does not permit the assembling of large sums of capital, the conducting of business on a grand scale and the elimination of the tremendous economic waste due to a certain kind of competition, is doomed to go. A railroad is, in its very nature, a "big business." At the beginning, when large individual fortunes were rare, few railroads indeed would have been built if there were no way of getting together comparatively small investors to cooperate, raise a large amount of capital, commensurate with the undertaking. For that purpose any other agency save a corporation would have been cumbersome and ill-adapted. A corporation can draw capital from tens of thousands of investors, assemble large sums

* The New Freedom, p. 180.

of money, engage in business on the grandest scale with the same efficiency and economy as if it consisted of the fewest number of investors permitted by law.

The limitation of risk is an essential ingredient of modern business organization. The *risk* to be discussed here is not the *relative risk* of corporation investors usually the theme of much controversy. It is to be understood here in a different sense.

The capitalist saw long ago the inadvisability of staking his entire fortune in one establishment. Business everywhere was so alluring that he yearned to have his finger in more pies than one. If he did not make out well in one enterprise he made up for it in another. Moreover, it gave the financier, the banker, an opportunity to take a hand in every business that could be manipulated to his own advantage. A controlling share in the business was all he needed, the rest might be distributed among thousands of small fry, for all he cared. Under individual proprietorship or partnership such practices would have been impossible. A failure in one partnership, the inability of the defunct business to meet all debts might mean the ruin of the rich partner. His investments in other business would not be immune from the claims of creditors. In a corporation, in case of failure, he is safe as far as his other investments are concerned. Capital must be free to move, invest itself all over the country, in all kinds of industry, in all parts of the world. Antiquated modes of business organization must not impede its mobility. Encumbrances and risks must be at a minimum.

Industry realized its needs and acted accordingly. If the corporate method is best suited to its development, it is selected as the prevailing mode of organization. It is the old principle of the survival of the fittest. There is no moralizing about it. The question of good or bad does not enter into the discussion at all. The corporation was most adaptable to the needs of the railroad business and it prevailed. To attack and rail against the "corporation," and consider it an evil in itself is folly; to understand it intelligently is important.

CHAPTER III

THE COMBINATION

If the first quarter of the nineteenth century is marked by the introduction of the corporate form of business organization, the last quarter of the century saw the birth of the trust, the syndicate, the pool, the holding company, the consolidation, the merger, the "agreements," the deals and private understandings of all kinds. Industry was unable longer to contain itself within the boundaries of the ordinary corporation. It sought to enlarge its business frontiers.

Rapid improvement in machinery gave rise to new instruments of transportation. New instruments of transportation and vastly improved conditions of travel facilitated communication. The phenomenal growth of industry and commerce have been both the effect and the cause of improved transportation.

Motive power has gone through several stages in development. While the advent of each successive *power* has meant greater efficiency, economy and speed, its introduction has been marked by many difficulties and much expense. The modest expenditures needed for the construction and equipment of a short-distance street railway is no longer sufficient. This is the age of Rapid Transit systems, steel cars, elaborate stations and gigantic power-houses. The initial expense for the construction of modern elevated and subway lines runs into hundreds of millions of dollars. Competition in a business requiring such great initial expenses is an absurdity. Combinations took root very rapidly.

During the great anti-trust wave which swept the country in the first decade of the twentieth century, the railroad business seemed to enjoy a quiet privilege. Politicians, legislators and journalists, trading on their anti-monopoly attitude, realized, less clearly at first but more and more so as the years rolled by, that the railroad business is in its very nature a monopoly. It has thereby been exempted from the general stigma attached to the industrial combination.

Railroads are distinct from most other business by reason of their public character. From the very beginning the railroad has been considered a public convenience. The right to engage in the railroad business requires more than the mere formal sanction of authority which corporations secure when about to engage in an ordinary industrial pursuit.

Whichever the railroad is to be, surface, elevated or subway, the company must get a special permit, known as a franchise. A street, a public thoroughfare is the result of a slow process of development and of the expense of much time, labor and money. The whole community contributes to its growth; the public thoroughfare is, therefore, the property of the whole community, a valuable property at that. To disfigure the street by laying rails on its surface, or to erect an elevated structure with its innumerable inconveniences, or to build a subway with its threatening danger to property and the necessary replacement of and interference with the various underground pipes and mains obviously requires special permission from the community. The considerations for these special rights and privileges and the methods the companies have employed in obtaining them will be discussed in chapter VII.

The outstanding fact is that once a franchise is granted to one company, for that particular route it has a practical monopoly. Moreover, if it is an important route, the numerous side routes and extensions are very often valuable only to that particular company. Some lines crossing sparsely populated sections are run at a small profit, at cost, or even at a slight loss by a company that has a transportation system in the heart of the city. It uses these lines as feeders. Only by taking the system as a whole do the lines become profitable enterprises. For other companies, each to run one of these lines independently would be suicidal. They would soon find themselves in the hands of receivers. Competition, on this score alone, is impossible.

And yet, there was competition or an attempt at competition in the early days of railroad development. So far as can be learned, the competition centered not so much in keeping rates down or in giving better service to the public, as in grabbing franchises.

The railroads learned the lesson of competition at a considerable price. The usual conditions prevailed. More companies were organized than could be profitably sustained. While on the surface things looked quiet and regular, underneath there raged a fierce struggle for existence. The companies possessing greater advantages in the struggle succeeded in crushing the weaker ones.

Of the amazingly large number of companies that were organized within the present limits of New York City to operate routes very few have remained alive and are doing business. And even the few apparently independent operating companies are controlled, in the final analysis, by a small group of financiers.

Darwin calculated that if one pair of elephants, the slowest breeders among mammals, were permitted to propagate their kind for 750 years, and if all the offspring lived and bred they would be the ancestors of nineteen million elephants. Luckily the struggle for existence kills a sufficient number of elephants to leave a little space in this world for the rest of us. So it is with the railroad companies. There have been so many of them organized in the short space of less than a century that, had they all lived and funcitoned we would now have a company for every 100 feet or so of railway. A ride in New York, such as we get now for five cents, would have been exceedingly expensive and fearfully annoying. Thanks to industrial progress we have been spared that agony.

Up to July 1, 1913, seven hundred and twenty-six corporations had been organized to operate routes in what is now New York City. More than two-thirds of these died, too weak to put up a fight, yielding to the inevitable without resistance. The 271 remaining companies struggled hard. They fought to survive, to be successful. After several years of warfare the battlegrounds, when cleared, found only 76 companies alive. The casualties were enormous, 195 out of 271 lost their identity. They were merged or foreclosed. Even the heroic 76 companies were not permitted to have the field all to themselves. Thirty-one of them chose to maintain a nominal existence only, leasing their properties to the remaining forty-five. These forty-five companies are further combined by means of the holding company. The few holding companies are, in turn, very effectually controlled by a small clique of financiers, trust companies, investing banks and insurance companies. The process of merging, consolidating and concentrating of control was phenomenal. There is a complete monopoly in the transit system of New York.

The "independent" holding companies entered into private agreements and understandings by which the city became completely helpless and entirely at their mercy. They divided the city into "spheres of influence," in which each combination is to reign supreme. They are doing on a small scale what financial imperialism does on a large scale.

How are these nefarious activities accomplished? How does this bear on the question of raising fares, and the entire tranction problem? Is it a product of our policy of ignorant indifference? If so, what should our policy be?

All these questions will be taken up in detail to indicate the *modus operandi* of the concentration of control of the traction business and its consequent deep-rooted evils to the community. We will explain briefly the "holy alliance" of financial monarchs, the intercorporate method of doing business.

CHAPTER IV

THE HOLY ALLIANCE

Intercorporate relations is a practice well known in the business world. It is a device by which common control is established. Separate companies are organized, but are all managed by the same directors. Separate corporations are maintained in spite of the duplicate expenses and obvious economic disadvantages because of the opportunities they offer for obtaining certain "rights" which may be permissible in law, but surely wrong in equity.

A glaring instance of such an arrangement designed to defraud the city was detected as far back as 1886. The Bleecker Street and Fulton Ferry Railroad Company and the Twenty-third Street Railroad Company were separate corporations, each having a franchise to operate a railway on a different route. The franchises were very valuable, and the Board of Aldermen, corrupt as that body was, did not dare to give them away entirely free. Agreements were made between the city and each of the companies whereby the city would be compensated for the franchises.

The Bleecker Street and Fulton Ferry Railroad Company was required to pay 1 per cent. of its gross receipts annually, while the 23rd Street R. R. Company paid a lump sum. By an agreement between the two companies to use certain tracks jointly the receipts were so mixed as to make it impossible to collect the assessments from the Bleecker Street and Fulton Ferry R. R. Company. In that way the city has been defrauded of tremendous sums of money annually.

The activities of a certain Jacob Sharp, of very shady connections, to obtain an additional franchise on the same terms as the above companies impelled the Mayor, who was in a row with the Board of Aldermen, to investigate the composition of the corporations. He found the same crowd controlling both companies by intercorporate directorates.*

Bleecker Street & Fulton Ferry R. R. Co.	*23rd St. R. R. Co.*
Pres. Jacob Sharp	Pres. Jacob Sharp
Sec. Thos. H. McLean	Sec. Thos. H. McLean
Treas. David J. King	Treas. Lewis May

* Meyer's History of Franchises in N. Y., p. 142.

DIRECTORS	DIRECTORS
J. Sharp	J. Sharp
Lewis May	Lewis S. Ballin
Eugene S. Ballin	Eugene S. Ballin
Isaak Hendrict	Isaak Hendrict
David James King	David James King
John Downey	John Downey
Henderson Moore	Henderson Moore
S. B. H. Vance	S. B. H. Vance
Thomas B. Rerr	L. Marx
Joseph Jacobs	Lazarus Rosenfeld
John H. Selmes	James Lynch
Alex. E. Kursheidt	John R. Flanagan
William Mangris	James Flanagan

Thus, two corporations, distinct in law were practically the same in fact. They were both steered and directed by the same hand.

Holy alliances between corporations, under more forms than one, exist with us to-day on a larger scale than ever and with more injurious effect.

When the appearance of independence no longer serves a "good" purpose, or when it is necessary to take some small and ill-reputed company under the protective wings of a larger corporation having back of it some great financier to enhance its credit, the companies fuse and assume the name of the favored corporation. Such a consolidation is called merger.

In the famous Metropolitan Street Railway Company merger, in 1895, the constituent members gave up their individuality. They gave up their names, their existence, and assumed a new name. The shareholders of the constituent dead members received shares from the new company, equivalent in amount to their previous holdings. Of course, the position of the creditors of the constituent companies was precisely the same as before the merger. It is a well-established principle in law that nothing the debtor will do can impair the rights of his creditors in law or in equity. The claim of the creditors is against the new corporation. It is, therefore, obvious that if the separate companies were mismanaged, wasteful and reckless in their financial dealings, and if they mortgaged their properties at a great price, and if they saddled the business with various bonded indebtedness bearing high rates of interest, the merger would not do away with these evils, for it assumes all the obligations of its members. It retains all the weaknesses of its constituent members; it does not establish the business on a solid financial basis.

The Metropolitan was just such a merger and, therefore, could not endure long. On November 19, 1907, a receiver was appointed to take charge of the properties.

The process of consolidation by merger became widespread. No fewer than 117 companies, organized to operate routes in New York, gave up their existence in merger.

The apparently innocuous trackage agreements and contracts for supplies and equipment are crowded with possibilities for fraud under intercorporate relations. It must be remembered always that the railroad companies are subject to regulation more or less, even if it be only the regulation of public opinion. Earnings must appear small, particularly so when employees demand higher wages, or when the public demands a reduction of fares, an extension of transfers, or when the companies demand an increase in fares.

Where intercorporate directorates exist trackage agreements, equipment contracts, leases—all offer a splendid opportunity for diverting profits into another company owned by the same crowd, as a "consideration" for certain "rights," supplies received, etc. In this way the expense of the company subject to regulation is bolstered up considerably. Then it is easy to plead poverty; more than that, prove it by "financial statements."

The Nassau Electric Railway Company, which absorbed 18 distinct railroad corporations by merger and controls many by leases, furnishes a classic example of manipulation designed to rob the public. On the surface there appears nothing wrong. Scratch the surface and the foul frauds become evident.

It should be noted that this company is completely controlled through stock ownership by the Brooklyn Rapid Transit Company. This control dates back to February 15, 1899.

The company owns power houses in various parts of New York and Brooklyn.

On February 28, 1907, the company leased its power houses to a corporation known as the Transit Development Company. On the same day its sister companies, all controlled by the Brooklyn Rapid Transit Company, joined it in leasing to the Transit Development Company their power houses and plants.

The Transit Development Company entered into an agreement with the companies of the

B. R. T. system whereby "the Development Company would take over and engage the employees and officers employed in these plants in connection with their operation, also to furnish all necessary labor and material for the maintenance and construction of track, sub and super structures, poles, wires and buildings, etc., as required by the several railroads companies, parties to this agreement."*

The same day the leases were made the Development Company entered into an agreement with its "landlords" to supply electrical power for the operation of their cars at the cost thereof, *plus 5 per cent.* This contract is commonly known as the "Power Consumption Contract."

The companies of the B. R. T. system were operating cars across the Brooklyn Bridge. Some time in 1907 they decided they wanted cars of a select type for local bridge service. On December 23, 1907, they entered into an agreement with their tenant, the Transit Development Company, to supply them with such cars and maintain them at operating efficiency, in consideration of which, the Development Company would re-

---

* Documentary History of Railroads, P. S. C. Reports for 1913, v. 5, p. 740.

ceive *all costs, plus* 10 *per cent.* Who is this fortunate Development Company? Why does it receive such fat contracts with guaranteed liberal profits? Is it in any way related to the B. R. T. Company?

The Transit Development Company is a corporation organized on April 22, 1902, for the following purposes:

"1. To purchase or otherwise acquire and hold, improve, operate, lease, rent, sell, grant and convey or exchange real property. . . .

"2. To carry on the business of general contractors, including the contracting with other corporations or persons for the supply of power or for the construction, equipment of railroads, bridges, wharfs, tunnels and subways, and carry out such contracts."*

The capital stock was to be $25,000 issued in one hundred dollar shares. From the minutes of a special meeting held by the company on October 14, 1902 at its offices at 168 Montague Street, Brooklyn, it appears that the B. R. T. Company is the sole owner of all of its capital, and, therefore, of the corporation itself. The

* From incorporation certificate.

affidavit attached to the minutes reads: "*I hereby certify* that the Brooklyn Rapid Transit Company is the holder of all the capital stock of Transit Development Company, and so appears on the books. . ."

The affidavit is signed by C. D. Meneley, secretary of Transit Development Company. Mr. Meneley is now the vice-president, member of the board and treasurer of the Brooklyn Rapid Transit Company.

Another affidavit attached to the minutes reads: "T. S. Williams, being duly sworn, says: That he is one of the directors of Transit Development Company and was present at a special meeting of the stockholders of the said company. . ."

Mr. Williams, up to the collapse, was the president, and at the time of the special meeting was the vice-president of the Brooklyn Rapid Transit Company.

The minutes are exceedingly absurd. The participants in the meeting go through the legal motions in real mock—serious fashion. Mr. Williams, as vice-president of the B. R. T. Company, the sole stockholder, pompously resolves that, "we, the undersigned, being all the stockholders of Transit

Development Company, together owning the entire capital stock of said company . . . do hereby authorize the directors of said company to hold . . . " a special meeting and do certain things. Whereupon, Mr. Williams, as director, in pursuance to instructions of Mr. Williams, "the stockholders" acts with extraordinary dispatch.

"On a motion, duly seconded, a vote was taken upon" a proposed resolution. "Thereupon, stockholders representing two hundred and fifty (250) shares of stock, being all of the capital stock of the said corporation, vote in favor of such resolution and no stockholders voted against this adoption, and thereupon such resolution was declared duly adopted and the meeting adjourned."

Mr. Williams acted the various roles in true Pooh-Bah style. All the stockholders were of "one mind" and therefore were unanimous in their decisions.

CHAPTER V

THE LEASE

Another instrument which has gained a foothold in our railroad system is the *lease*. It is an arrangement whereby one corporation transfers the right to possession and use of its properties to another corporation. It differs from a sale in that the title to the property remains with the original owner. The owner of the property is called lessor, landlord; the user of the property is called lessee, tenant. Under the lease the well-known relations of landlord and tenant exist.

There are many reasons why railroad companies prefer the lease instead of the sale, particularly when the landlord and tenant are the same party; and if traced back far enough they are usually found to be the same. In the case of a sale, if it is genuine, the purchaser scrutinizes carefully the value of the property. He does not voluntarily pay for watered stock. He does not assume heavy bonded indebtedness. He takes a physical valuation of the road and pays what competent appraisers in his employ tell him to pay. If the sale is not genuine, some such procedure would have to be followed if only to keep up appearances; otherwise, the purchase would be a fraud too plain to be concealed. The consideration in a sale is a lump sum.

The lease is different. The consideration for a lease is usually in installment sums, in rentals. The lessee takes over the roads as they are, with all encumbrances and obligations. He pays an interest on the bonded indebtedness, taxes, salaries of officers and all expenses required by the lessor company. In addition, the tenant usually agrees to pay dividends to the landlord's stockholders. As a rule the dividends are fixed. They become part of the "expenses" of the operating company.

Thus, the Interborough Rapid Transit Company, whose president is so vociferous in his demand for a higher fare, giving the poverty of the company as a reason, pays to its landlords, the Manhattan Railway Company, "guaranteed dividends—7 per cent. on Manhattan Railway Company capital stock," amounting annually to the enormous sum of $4,200,000.* And yet the company claims it pays no dividends. Besides these guaranteed dividends the Interborough Rapid Transit Company pays:

* Annual Report of the I. R. T. Co. for 1918, p. 5.

*Interest on Manhattan Railway Consolidated mortgage 4% bonds....	$1,627,360
Interest on Manhattan Railway 2nd mortgage 4% bonds...........	180,920
Manhattan Railway (organization).	35,000
Total	$1,843,280

The Manhattan Railway Company has an interesting history. Almost from its very birth, December 29, 1875, it struggled to overcome the opposition of two other companies, the New York Elevated Company and the Metropolitan Elevated Railroad Company. By various arrangements, litigations and schemes the Manhattan Railway Company absorbed the other two completely.

"January 1, 1903, this company leased its property and franchises to Interborough Rapid Transit Company, the lease to take effect from April 1, 1903, and to run for a period of 999 years from November 1, 1875. The lease provided for a nominal rent of $10,000 and guaranteed to the stockholders on the Manhattan Com-

* **Annual Report of the I. R. T. Co. for 1918, p. 5.**

pany an amount equal in the aggregate to not exceed 7 per cent. on that company's stock, and to be not less than 6 per cent. and, after January 1, 1906, 7 per cent.; the Interborough to pay as rent also the interest of outstanding debenture bonds of the New York Elevated Railroad Company to the amount of $1,000,000, also the interest on $10,818,000 first mortgage bonds on the Metropolitan Elevated Railroad Company, and on $28,065,000 consolidated mortgage bonds of the Manhattan Railway Company, and of all bonds to be issued; the lessee to pay all taxes and charges of a like nature."*

The Interborough pays the staggering sum of $6,000,000 annually, of which more than two-thirds is pure profit, the rest being interest to the Manhattan Company for 999 years. Capitalism takes a long lease unto itself, it figures without its host, the people.

From April 1, 1903, to April 1, 1919, according to the lease, the Interborough has already paid to the Manhattan Company $67,200,000 in net profits, a sum many times the actual value of the roads. If the present disgraceful partnership between the city and the Interborough, of which

* P. S. C. Reports, 1st Dist., 1913, v. 5, p. 664.

more later, is allowed to run to the end, the public will be obliged to pay to the Manhattan Company, through the Interborough, about $205,800,000 in net profits.

President Shonts complains his company is not able to pay dividends. Does he deliberately overlook $6,000,000 which go annually and, if he has it his way, will continue to go for 955 years longer to the Manhattan Company? When he speaks of dividends, does he not know that as far as the people are concerned, dividends paid under the name of "rentals" or any other name are dividends none the less?

Another interesting case of manipulation by means of the *lease* is the Bridge Operating Company. This company was organized May 21, 1904, for the purpose of operating local cars on the surface tracks of Williamsburg Bridge at a fare of three cents for a single ticket and five cents for two trips. The company was organized by the B. R. T. Company and the New York City Railways Company. Its capital stock was to be $100,000 to be sold in 1,000 shares at $100 per share.

The B. R. T. Company and the New York

City Railways Company each agreed to take 500 shares and pay for them in cash, at par. Other stipulations in the agreement seemed to show that the two companies were to be equal partners in this new corporation.

June 21, 1907, the Bridge Operating Company leased its properties to the Brooklyn Heights Railway Company and the New York City Railway Company. In consideration for this the two "tenants" were to assume all obligations and duties of the "landlord" and guarantee six per cent. dividends to the landlord's stockholders, which in this case are no other than the tenants themselves.

By a "gentleman's agreement" one of the tenants, the New York City Railway Company, left the operation of the leased properties to its partner for a consideration, of course. "It seems that actual operation of the Local Bridge service was at once assumed by the Brooklyn Heights Railroad Company and has ever since that date been carried on exclusively by that company. By an exchange of letters it has apparently been agreed that the Brooklyn Heights Company shall receive $5,000 a year for general administration of the line and $2,500 a year for depot, storage and shop facilities. . . ."*

According to its annual report for 1918, the Brooklyn Rapid Transit Company is in complete control through stock ownership of the Brooklyn Heights Railway.

For all practical purposes these transactions are reduced to this: The B. R. T. Company organizes a corporation, allows it to live an independent life for a little less than three years, in which time it is made to acquire certain valuable franchises, it is made to enter into contracts and agreements, then it is made to lease all "its" rights and possessions to the B. R. T. Company. As the Bridge Operating Company, the B. R. T. is a landlord receiving rent and a six per cent. guaranteed dividend; as the Brooklyn Heights, the B. R. T. is a tenant cheerfully paying rent to its landlord.

This absurd double role acted by one and the same company successfully to conceal profits may not have been tolerated in a less enlightened age, but in modern times it is perfectly good business. The accepted business ethics seems to be: If you get away with it, you are entitled to it.

* P. S. C. Reports, 1st Dist., 1909, v. II, p. 130.

The excessive rentals paid by the Brooklyn Rapid Transit Company are no mean contribution towards its insolvency. The reasons for the financial "failure" are not to be sought in the low fares —for they are not low at all; in fact they are too high—but in obscure transactions, such as these leases present. To pay large dividends under the guise of rentals, and at the same time plead poverty, is little short of criminal fraud. But this is the very thing that is artfully practiced by the traction trust.

The Brooklyn City Railroad Company, one of the "landlords" of the Brooklyn Rapid Transit Company, received annually as large a dividend as 10 per cent. upon its capital stock, not to exceed $12,000,000, and interest on its bonded indebtedness, not to exceed $6,925,000, all charges of maintenance, taxes, etc., besides.

"May 14, 1893, the company leased its entire road to the Brooklyn Heights Railroad Company for 999 years from June 6, 1893, the date when the lease took effect. . . The lessee agreed to pay to the company an annual rental at the rate of 10 per cent. per annum upon the outstanding capital stock of the company, not to exceed $12,000,000, and the interest on the bonded indebtedness of the company not to exceed $6,925,000. All charges for maintenance, taxes, etc., were to be paid by the lessee. The lessee agreed, moreover, not to reduce the fare charged on the road."*

Thus, it appears, the Brooklyn City Company has received annually *in pure profits* the sum of $1,200,000 since June 6, 1893, making a total up to date of $31,200,000. This is another case where the people have already paid in pure profit a sum sufficient to pay for the entire capital stock of the company more than two and a half times over and still the roads remain the property of the corporation with the right to draw $1,200,000 annually for 973 years longer or, in the aggregate, the stupendous sum of $1,167,600,000!

That it is absurd for a corporation capitalized at $12,000,000 to draw a guaranteed profit of $1,198,800,000 does not alter the fact that *this is the lease, the sacred contract* to which the people have already given sanction and reality by paying $31,200,000 without a protest. Whether they will continue to do so, by raising fares if necessary, depends wholly on how intelligently they understand the problem.

It should be remembered that these guaran-

* P. S. C. Reports, 1st Dist., 1913, v. 5, pp. 180-181.

teed dividends are payments made in addition to all expenses and obligations of the "leased" property, no matter how much it has been swelled, and are to be deducted from the gross earnings of the lessor. These rentals are not listed in the financial statements as profits or dividends, but rather as fixed charges. Yet, what are these rentals if not dividends in disguise?

The abuses here cited, practiced by means of the *lease*, will furnish a bare glimpse of what is going on behind the curtains of our traction systems. The extent of concealed profits made by these methods alone will become clear when it is realized that 31 companies in greater New York are operated under leases, the terms of which range between 99 and 999 years. The most important of them are for periods of 999 years.

CHAPTER VI

THE HOLDING COMPANY

Intimately connected with the *lease* is the *holding company*. It is the latest form of combination. A holding company is a corporation having exclusive or part powers to purchase and hold stock of other corporations. By acquiring a majority interest in the stock of many corporations or an amount sufficient to give it a controlling interest, the holding company becomes the dictator of the policies, financial and otherwise, of its members. In that way, although maintaining nominal independence and a separate existence, most of the railway companies in New York City are controlled by a very few individuals, invisible, relentless, greedy and indifferent to the public interest.

The holding company is the combine of combines. It is of recent origin. It sprang into prominence soon after the United States Supreme Court handed down the decisions (1890-1892) in the Oil and Sugar Trusts, declaring the trust form of industrial combination illegal. Industrial development, however, decreed that business should combine, the decisions of the courts to the contrary notwithstanding. And business did combine.

If one form of organization is declared illegal another will be devised. When the trust was "busted" the legal acumen constantly at the elbow of big business immediately found a new scheme, the holding company, a combination no less effectual, no less monopolistic, no less given to possible abuse than the trust. This, the lawyers said, was a legal method because a corporation has a right to hold property, and stock is property. The courts, at first, upheld this view unreservedly.

The public utility corporations, particularly, are afflicted with the disease of the holding company. Due to the fact that they are generally accepted as being natural monopolies, the railroad combines have not been subjected to as much legislative hindrance or moral disapprobation on the part of the public as have the industrial combinations. Taking full advantage of this partial immunity, the traction trust has known no bounds in its spoliation.

"The total capital employed in electric, gas, street, and interurban railway companies, commonly called Public Utility Corporations, in this country to-day is estimated to exceed *eight billion dollars*, and of this capital nearly *five and one-half billion dollars* are controlled by holding companies and their subsidiary companies. . . .

"Street and interurban railway companies represent a total capital approximately *five billion dollars.* Of this sum it is estimated that *not less than two-thirds is controlled by holding companies.* In the 28 cities of the United States having a population in excess of 2,000,000 the mileage of track controlled by holding companies is in excess of 61 per cent. Here, again, it is of interest to note that only four of these cities have more than one principal operating company and only two of these cities have companies that are really independently and separately owned."*

These holding companies fall into two groups.

1. Those which own stock in other corporations and also operate routes of their own. Such are the Third Avenue Railway Company and the New York Railways Company. Holding companies operating routes themselves are called parent companies; the corporations whose stock is held are known as subsidiary companies.

* From a brief submitted on behalf of public utility holding companies to the Interstate Commerce Committee of the United States Senate, in the matter of Senate Bill No. 4160—reprinted in Gerstenberg's "Material of Corporation Finance," pp. 571-572.

2. Those created solely for the purpose of owning stock in other companies. They own in order to control; and are only administrative in their function. Such are the Brooklyn Rapid Transit Company and the Interborough Consolidated Corporation.

The holding companies are gigantic in scope. They exercise a decidedly monopolistic control over scores of corporations.

In "the Brooklyn Rapid Transit Company system no fewer than 83 companies are represented. Of these 83 companies, 67 have lost their identity through absorption, leaving but 16 distinct companies. Of these 16 companies, 9 are operated under lease or agreement by other companies, thus leaving but seven operating companies. The seven operating companies are subject to a common control through a single company, the Brooklyn Rapid Transit Company."*

The Interborough Consolidated Corporation is a pure and unadulterated holding company. It exists solely for the purpose of controlling two of the largest systems of roads in New York, which are themselves holding companies. It controls the Interborough Rapid Transit Company, by own-

* Preface, P. S. C. Reports, First Dist., 1913, v. 5.

ing $33,812,800 worth of capital stock out of the company's total capital stock of $35,000,000; it controls the New York Railways Company by owning $15,276,558.20 worth of capital stock of the company's total capital stock of $17,495,-060. These two systems have issued *hundreds of millions of dollars* worth of bonds, and carry almost half of all the passengers using local transportation in New York. The Interborough Consolidated Corporation is the largest holding company of its kind.

A clear realization of how completely the three holding companies, the Third Avenue Railway Company, the Brooklyn Rapid Transit Company and the Interborough Consolidated Corporation control the transportation system in Greater New York, may be seen by referring to the three charts appended to Vol. II. of the Annual Report of the Public Service Commission for 1916.

The economic advantages of combination, unified control for the purpose of carrying on business on a large scale, elimination of duplicate service, duplicate overhead charges, etc., is not furnished by the holding company; there is no scientific unified management of the roads themselves although there is plenty of unity in the control of their financial policy; in fact, there is more unity of that kind of control than is good for the public. The holding company, as far as the people are concerned, is an instrument creating a complete monopoly of an indispensable public necessity in the hands of a few financiers. It retains all the disadvantages and evils of a combination without giving the compensating advantages.

Back of the holding company are bankers, trust companies, insurance companies and such other public benefactors. Their purpose in owning the stock of the roads is not so much the collection of dividends, although this, too, is quite a consideration, but the large earnings which figure as expenses on the financial sheet but are in fact profits. This could not be successfully accomplished save through intercorporate control, such as the holding company creates. There are financial loans to be made by the subsidiary companies in which the financiers and other investing interests are vitally interested. They secure for themselves most favorable terms as bond holders. There are those fat underwriting fees, promoters' fees, organization fees, which run into millions of dollars with every reorganization scheme of any of the large companies. These fees, when paid, are charged to the cost of the road. Such was the case in the reorganization of the Metropolitan Street Railway. Over $4,000,000 were spent on those items. Such was the case when the Interborough was raising money when it entered into the famous contract with the city in 1913.

It is an old practice for the banker-director to make terms upon which he, as banker, would advance money to the corporation of which he is an influential director. This dual capacity of the director makes the corporation a source of constant sapping for the financier. Louis D. Brandeis, now Justice of the United States Supreme Court, says:

"A large part of these underwriting commissions is taken by the great banking houses, not for their services in selling the bonds, nor in assuming risks. Thus, when the Interborough Railway—a most prosperous corporation—financed its recent $170,000,000 bond issue, J. P. Morgan & Co. received a 3 per cent. commission, that is, $5,100,000, practically for arranging that others should underwrite and sell the bonds."*

The financiers could not obtain such stupendous

* Other People's Money, by Louis D. Brandeis, p. 96.

sums of easy money with so little difficulty if they did not immediately control those who control the holding company which, in turn, controls the corporations.

The money loaned to pay these fees and interest thereon are to be amortized out of the fares collected. Is there any wonder the corporations are "losing money" on a five-cent fare?

CHAPTER VII

FRANCHISES

HOW THEY ARE OBTAINED

The future generation, looking at the remains of the haphazard lay-out of our transportation lines, will say with a great deal of sympathy and no little contempt: "What savages our ancestors were! They should be pitied for having lived in a world so wasteful, so unscientific and so inconvenient." This would be the verdict of any sensible person not accustomed to the helter-skelter of New York life, who would take the trouble to traverse this city. There is no system to our street railways and scarcely any in our elevated lines and subways. If rails, properly separated, were thrown from the clouds to fall at random in New York streets there could hardly have been more confusion than there is to-day.

One of the principal reasons for this state of affairs is the blind ignorance and corruption of a certain class of politicians who have ruled this city on and off for the past one hundred years. They have had neither the intelligence nor the will to perceive the city's needs. There has been no definite policy, no guiding principle by which the affairs of the city were conducted any more than there is to-day.

The chaotic and anarchic condition of our railway facilities is not due to blind natural forces or mere accident; on the contrary, it is the result of conscious consent of authority. No railway can be built without a special permission, without a franchise.

"Franchises," says Chief Justice Taney, of the United States Supreme Court, "are special privileges conferred by government upon individuals, and which do not belong to the citizens of the country generally of common right."*

There are four kinds of franchises—perpetual, limited-term, short-term, and indeterminate. A perpetual franchise is one which is granted forever. It is irrevocable. The grantee becomes vested of a right in the street of which he cannot be deprived; and it does not matter if the grant was obtained by questionable means. That it is an absurdity for one generation to grant away the rights of posterity is no concern of the law.

The limited-term franchise is one granted for a definite time, at the expiration of which the com-

* Bank of Augusta v. Earle, 13 Peters, 519-595.

munity is re-invested with the rights it had given away. A limited-term is considered a period of between 99 to 999 years. To all intents and purposes a 999-year term is perpetual. Most street franchises in New York are either outright perpetual or for a "limited-term" of 999 years.

A short-term franchise is one granted for a period ranging from 10 to 99 years. Such grants are looked upon with great disfavor by all sides, because it prevents good service to the public and is of no special value to the corporations.

The indeterminate franchise is one, the duration of which is uncertain, depending upon the behavior of the company as well as the policy of the municipality. It is a tenure during good behavior, as it were. Such franchises usually provide that the city has a right at any time it so decides to take over the properties upon paying the then fair value thereof exclusive of the franchise. An indeterminate franchise presupposes government regulation.

What gives a man or group of men a superior right, or as is more accurately designated, a privilege to use a street to the practical exclusion of others? How do a few individuals obtain these "rights" to capitalize a common need of a people of a city, own and use it for their private profit?

The history of franchises in New York is the darkest chapter in municipal history. If one wishes to learn how much of a corrupting influence private ownership subject to governmental control is; if one desires to fathom to what depths of criminal practices politicians will sink and how far they permit themselves deliberately to betray their constituencies; if one wishes to chill his faith in the "rule of the people," let him delve into the mire of franchise history in New York. Dr. Mila Roy Maltbie, once a member of the Public Service Commission, and probably its ablest member since its inception, in summarizing a "History of Franchises in New York City," says:

"The preceding pages reek with instance upon instance of corruption and robbery of the city, but the half has not been told. If only the evidence had been presented which is to be found in court records and proceedings of legislative investigations, to say nothing of well substantiated reports and the vast Augean stables closed to public eyes, the reader would rebel and throw aside the nauseating narrative. *Indeed, one is almost convinced* *that not a single franchise in New York City, with the exception possibly of many wharf and ferry privileges, has been gained without corrupt means.*"* This leads one to ponder well whether the claim may not be true, which is made by ardent supporters of municipalization, that private control of franchises almost surely leads to corruption, and that with all their official corruption and dishonesty conditions would not have been and would not be as bad, if municipal ownership were adopted, as under private ownership."†

Long before the first railroad franchise was granted, in 1832, the need of transportation facilities more adequate than the stage coach could furnish, became imperative. In spite of the bright prospects for profits in railroad investments capitalists stood aloof.

In the first place, industrial investments were so remunerative that capital was not anxious to venture into a new and doubtful field. Capitalists do not make investments out of a desire to serve the community. Their motive is profits.

In the second place, they held back in order

* Italics are mine.

† History of Franchises, Gustavus Myers, p. 200.

to secure the maximum advantages. The argument, so familiar to all was used then as it is now: Capital is timid, it needs encouragement. The people were so skillfully played upon that they began to view the prospective railroad investor as a great public benefactor. He was a heroic soul ready to make all sacrifices for the people. He was the industrial explorer discovering strange and hitherto unknown fields. In true appreciation for his devotion to the community, the man seeking to build a railroad was given every opportunity to accomplish his purpose. He was given the public streets free, no rights were reserved for adequate regulations, no time limit was set to his privilege to keep the streets; he was even granted special subsidies.

Meanwhile, the city was growing by leaps and bounds. The influx of foreigners was enormous. The political upheavals and famines in Europe, coupled with the introduction of the steamship about that time, making water transportation safer, speedier and cheaper, accellerated greatly the immigration to our shores. According to the Federal census the population of Manhattan Island increased from 60,489 in 1800 to 615,000 in 1850, to 942,000 in 1870.

The first railroad lines built proved to be very successful. The profits were enormous. There was a scramble for franchises. Though the public was slow in realizing the value of its streets, the politicians were not. They discovered that a franchise will command a price.

A new kind of politician sprang into existence. His sole purpose in seeking election was to be able to sell franchises. He looked upon his vote in the Board of Aldermen, by which franchises were granted, as his private property, and had a right to sell it; in fact, what he was selling was not public franchises at all, but his private vote, and, therefore, committed no grave wrong. Bribing aldermen became the common thing. It was as conventional and natural for an alderman to accept a bribe as it was for the Russian administrators under the Czar.

Year after year men with heavy clouds of suspicion hanging over them, belonging to an organization recognized as the public school of corruption—Tammany Hall—were returned to office to "govern" the city. Towards the end of 1852, rumors of rampant corruption and bribery in the City Council were rife. The thieves fell out among themselves, and, as usual, the truth came to light. From an affidavit by a James A. Coulter, a lobbyist, a man of the inside, the public learned of the existence of thoroughly organized agencies "to receive and distribute bribe money." On February 26th, 1853, the grand jury, after a careful investigation, reported that Aldermen received bribes for granting various franchises, and continued:

"It was clearly shown that enormous sums of money had been expended for and towards the procurement of railroad grants in the city, and that towards the decisions and procurement of the Eighth Avenue railroad grant a sum so large that would startle the most credulous, was expended, but, in consequence of the voluntary absence of important witnesses, the grand jury was left without direct testimony of the particular recipients of the different amounts."*

Such exposes were frequent. Every once in a while the people would be mortally shocked by some foul act of their representatives. The city would rock with indignation.

---

* Documents of the Board of Aldermen, XXI, Part II, No. 55—quoted in Myer's History of Franchises, p. 116.

Unfortunately for democracy, the people have extremely short memories. Moved by a wave of temporary excitement they defeat the misdemeanants, organize some nondescript fusion ticket and sweep it into office. Before long the would-be reformers, permeated by a large amount of the old stock, become deformers; they find the job of bartering away the people's interests very profitable. They usually out-tammany Tammany.

Things would become so bad that the people began to long for the good old days. At the same time Tammany Hall, the "bad man" in politics, puts on the garment of virtue, gets unto itself some "clean" leader, a "servant of the people," re-enters the political fight, and, with the aid of the dead and the babies, all of whom are registered and voting, with the aid of stuffed boxes, and such other political acts as are deemed necessary, the "clean" candidate is "victorious." This has been a repeated performance in New York politics since the day when the memory of man runneth not to the contrary.

By 1860 the Legislature, moved by a feeling— on the part of some to relieve the people of New York City from the irreparable injury being done to them by a pack of organized crooks, and on the part of others, by sheer envy at the lucrative profits made by the Aldermen—passed a law taking away from the council the power of granting franchises, and vesting it exclusively in itself. Conditions were so bad in the city government in those days that there was not a murmur of protest from any source against these violations of home rule, except, of course, from the City Council itself, which felt aggrieved at being deprived of such a valuable source for private enrichment. It looked upon the Legislature as its foremost business competitor.

The people chose the lesser of two evils. To permit the Legislature, sitting over one hundred miles away from the city and composed of representatives from all over the state, to regulate the streets in New York was deplorable; but, reasoned the people, at least it will be an honest regulation; if by reason of its distance from the city the Legislature errs in some things, it was preferable to being constantly sold out and deliberately betrayed by a corrupt Council at home.

What a smashing disappointment and terrible disillusion this was! Within a month of the passage of the act the franchise lobbyists, railroad advocates, promoters and schemers removed their seat of operation to Albany. They beseiged the capital. Trained in the art of lobby warfare, encouraged by years of victory, equipped with the most poisonous weapon—gold—the invading New York hoards overwhelmed the weaklings stationed at the Albany post to guard the interest of the people. The Legislature shamefully surrendered.

Dozens of bills granting franchises to rival companies were introduced. The flames consuming honest government at the City Hall enveloped the capitol and reduced the good name of the State to ashes. The legislators were even more brazen and crooked, if such a thing were possible, than the Aldermen. Criticism by the Governor was listened to with impatience and contempt. They took to graft as hungry wolves take to their prey.

Five franchises, which, with the possible exception of Broadway, constituted the most valuable remaining thoroughfares in the city, estimated at that time to be worth between fifteen to twenty million dollars, were delivered to speculators and railroad sharks almost without any compensation.

"It was generally believed that the passage of these five bills cost the projectors $250,000 in money and stock, distributed among the purchasable members of the two houses of the Legislature. Some persons, who profess to know, put the cost of one-half million dollars."*

Competition brought down the price of an assemblyman's vote considerably. The Board of Aldermen maintained a much higher standard. Between $300 and $400 was all an assemblyman was to receive for his vote on a Broadway bill, a franchise which later netted $22,000 to each Alderman for his vote. Besides the unpardonable fault of selling their votes too cheaply, upstate legislators measured up well to the standards of "honesty" set by New York representatives. They were not all averse to accepting bribes for voting away New York City's rights. Republicans were no different than Democrats. The latter had no monopoly on corruption. Lobbyists generally agreed that it did not matter who was elected, for it cost less to buy a legislator than to elect one.

On April 23, 1863, the Broadway railroad bill came up for final passage. Charm and dignity were lent to the proceedings and deliberations when the august statesmen were made aware of

* History of Franchises, Gustavus Myers, pp. 124-125.

the presence of police, who came to the chamber to enforce the law against the lawmakers.

"About 9 o'clock an officer of the city police court appeared in the lobby with a large number of subpoenas, addressed to members of the house and gentlemen of the lobby, from which it appeared proceedings of some sort had been commenced in that court against Speaker Callicot, the precise character of which seemed to be known to no one.

"Up to midnight an intense excitement prevailed, and the officer in question continued to search for those whose whereabouts could not be ascertained. It was finally concluded on all hands that the proceedings were nothing more or less than a strategic movement having reference solely to the Broadway bill. . . ."*

The next day, only one day before the time set for adjournment, marked by the usual confusion and disorder of the adjournment of the August legislature, "the final vote was taken amid vehement charges of corruption and all sorts of unworthy influences."†

This intolerable condition kept up unabated

---

* Albany dispatch, New York *Times* April 23, 1863.
† Albany dispatch, New York *Times*, April 24, 1863.

until 1874. The constitutional convention, held that year, incorporated a provision in the Constitution to the effect that no franchises might be granted without the consent of the local authorities and half the owners of property along the contemplated route, failing the latter, the consent of the General Term of the Supreme Court. This amendment was adopted by the people and went into effect January 1, 1875. It was a rebuke administered to the Legislature by a resentful people for the shameful betrayal of the people's trust.

The limitations placed by law on the Legislature's powers were such as to make it almost impossible to grant a franchise in New York without making a bargain with the City Council. As a result, for nine years, all attempts at passing railway grant bills, except the Rapid Transit Act of 1875, proved futile.

In 1884 a law was passed again giving the local authorities the power to grant railway franchises. The promoters and speculators worked zealously for its passage. The same year, the Board of Aldermen granted away what was at that time the most valuable franchise in the city, the right to run a railroad on Broadway. The battle to "get Broadway," the street considered at that time as the pride and the key of New York, raged for over twenty years. The history of the Broadway franchise battle, both in the Legislature and City Council, abounds with criminal incidents. There were many competitors for this prize.

As far back as May of that year "deals" were entered into between the Aldermen and the companies on a resolution to be voted on August 6th. Each competitor company offered a large compensation for the franchise, not to the city of course, but to the Aldermen. The price an Alderman received for his vote was unusually high $22,000.

Happily there were too many conflicting interests in this affair to permit full secrecy. The truth leaked out. The Aldermen were indicted and convicted. Three Aldermen, Duffy, Fullgraff and Waite, turned state's evidence. Some of the sentences imposed by Recorder Smythe were as high as nine years and ten months. At the trial before Recorder Smythe, on November 19th, 1886, Alderman Fullgraff (significant name!), testified thus:

"A special meeting of the Board was held in

my factory, on Fulton Street, in the month of May, 1884. There were thirteen members present. They were, De Lacy, Dempsey, McLoughlin, Sayles, McQuade, McCabe, Kenney, Jaehne, Cleary, Reilly, O'Neill, Duffy and myself. It was proposed that the thirteen vote together on everything that came up except on political issues.

"It was determined to have a meeting at McLoughlin's house a week later. At this meeting the same thirteen were present. The first subject taken up was the Broadway franchise. It was stated that a cable railroad company had applied for the privilege. It was said that the company had offered $750,000, half cash and half bonds, and that the Broadway Company had offered $500,000 in cash. I think Jaehne said that the acceptance of the $750,000 would be risky, as the bonds could be traced. He thought the Broadway Surface people would be safer."*

The irony of this unspeakable crime is that the law, the violation of which resulted in sending the thieves to long terms at hard labor, protected the criminals in their theft; it gave them the franchise. Although it was charged and proven that the Aldermen received bribes for voting the way

* Quoted in Myer's History of Franchises, p. 139.

they did, yet the public rights they gave away were binding upon the city forever. Although it was charged and proven that Jacob Sharp and friends to whom the grant was given corrupted the Board of Aldermen by paying to its members large bribes, yet the grant which they thus obtained could not be taken away from them. That is the law!

When the matter of annulling the stolen franchise came to the court, it held that the grant, the interest in the streets, was perpetual and indefeasible; that it was a vested interest, and the directors must act as trustees for the creditors and shareholders.

The plain people may not fully comprehend how a "right" obtained by corruption and fraud can become "vested," but then they do not know the fine points of the law. The only danger in this decision is that the people are likely to assign to all "vested interests" a criminal and fraudulent origin. Such a feeling, taking root among the people, will do more to undermine the "foundation of modern society" than thousands of Socialist speeches.

A fruitful source of revelations of corruption and graft was the exceptionally low depth to which the Aldermen sank. They even failed to observe the "honor" observed among thieves. They became extremely undependable. They accepted bribes from one company to vote for its project, then they would accept money from its competitors to betray the former. They would award the franchise to the highest bidder, but they would accept both bids.

It is needless to go into further details to show the manner in which railroad franchises were obtained in New York City. Suffice it to say that the grounds upon which the companies established their "vested rights" in the New York streets are invalid; their successors must be treated as recipients of stolen goods with complete knowledge of the facts; their title is, from every point of view, faulty. The people will some day demand a return of their stolen possessions.

CHAPTER VIII

STEALING THE "UNDERGROUND HOLE"

SUBWAY CONTRACTS OF 1900-1902

Very few people know that New York City, the metropolis of the world, owns the greater and most important part of its transit facilities, the subway system. Still fewer people know that there was a referendum on the question and that the citizens cast an overwhelming vote in favor of municipal ownership. It is not strange that they do not know, for, although the people voted for municipal ownership, although the city spent hundreds of millions of dollars in building a rapid transit system, the authorities lack courage, willingness and intelligence to make municipal ownership a fact in the life of our city. Not only that, but they used the opportunity presented by the vote for municipal ownership as a cloak for one of the greatest steals in the history of our city up to that time.

The first subway contracts known in official language as contracts Nos. 1 and 2, are robberies committed mid-day, in full view of all. Compared to this all previous private acquisitions of the city's possessions are mild and unimportant. The curious thing is that in the consummation of these infamous contracts, the devil managed to bring together the well-meaning but short-sighted reformer, the cunning financier and the vicious politician. Considering who the midwives were it is to be marvelled that the offspring is not actually worse than it is.

For a number of years after their construction, in the eighties, the elevated railroads were ample and satisfactory as rapid transit facilities. They offered complete relief from the intolerable congestion existing prior to their advent. Like all things it carried within itself the elements of its own destruction. By opening up new areas for residential purposes it laid the foundation for a greater congestion.

With the constant and feverish growth of the city, the industrial centers and the residential sections grew apace. In some cases people spent extremely unpleasant hours in their daily travel to and from their daily work. Mere inconvenience soon became an intolerable burden. People were herded like cattle into suffocating cars with no adequate seating capacity. Only one taking the Brooklyn-bound elevated train on the Brooklyn Bridge in the six o'clock rush hour can fully appreciate the agony and feeling of the people at that time. The daily traveller began to view the transportation facilities of the city as a hell on earth. Demands were made with increasing persistence for better and more rapid transit. Rapid transit was the issue of the hour.

The elevated railroads, the rapid transit of yesterday, became the horse-car of to-day. Having covered the surface, having gone into the air, the next step in quest for relief was the "underground hole."

One of the greatest weaknesses in the structure of our government is its irresponsiveness to the will and need of the people. It takes the authorities years before any popular demand is satisfied. Officials move inconveniently slow.

Long delays result in increasing popular pressure. A point is reached when action must be taken in haste to appease popular indignation. Things done in haste are seldom done well.

Public needs held back until they become pressing, is good politics. What cannot be accomplished when people are frantic about something!

Vicious and discredited political organizations are swept into power for "championing the cause." When in power the condition of immediate necessity, action in a hurry is a justification for all sorts of vicious designs to do evil.

In 1891, the State Legislature, in pursuance to a strong popular demand, enacted a Rapid Transit Act* providing for the appointment of a Board of Rapid Transit Commissioners to investigate whether the public interest required the construction of an underground rapid transit railway, and if they found it did, to lay out the routes, establish plans for constructions, get the necessary consents, and sell at public auction the privilege of constructing the road, and operate it for a stated number of years. All public offers to sell this franchise for a "limited-term" of 999 years proved futile. Only one bidder, said to have been irresponsible, appeared. He offered a ridiculously small sum as compensation to the city, and the bid was rejected. There seemed to be a conspiracy not to pay anything for the greatest of all franchises. Why pay when it was reasonably certain that the companies could get it for nothing, if they waited? And they waited.

* Chapter 4, Laws of 1891.

Those who proposed selling railroad franchises at auction as the final remedy against public loot, once again, and for the last time, saw how successfully their ideas failed. The "ring" was not to be outwitted or outdone by auctions. Responsible railroad companies would not bid. There was no competition to secure the most profitable system of railroads! Private understandings among the railroad interests are as effective and binding as if they were bound by a sealed agreement.

They declared an "open strike." With the intolerable congestion unrelieved the "open strike," the "folding of arms" on the part of the capitalists, their refusal to invest in the building of new lines, was bound to succeed. Such power in the hands of an extremely small group of people, who do not hesitate to use it in holding up the city, is dangerous.

When street cleaners or policemen employed by the city, fold their arms and demand decent human conditions and a living wage, they are declared to be outlaws. The wrath of the "public" is upon them. The entire power of the government is used to crush the "arrogance" of the men who engage in a "hold-up" of the city. But when the railroad financiers refuse to build roads in order to press the city against the wall, compel it to grant most favorable concessions, hold up the traveling public who have no option but to use the roads, for fabulous profits, they are not declared outlaws; in fact, they are held out as the most patriotic and "best people" in the community.

The first four years the Rapid Transit laws of 1891 were a dead letter. They were years crowded with discontentment. Abuses multiplied in profusion, congestion on cars was growing worse. The people were prepared to go to extremes to get relief.

In the confusion the reformers got on the job and gained a footing. They usually fish in muddy waters. Former Mayor Hewitt, a staunch advocate of municipal ownership of railroads—a certain kind of municipal ownership, got on the job. In 1894, the Chamber of Commerce, of which Mr. Hewitt was a member and the moving spirit, drafted a bill and had it introduced in the Legislature providing for municipal ownership of roads, which should be leased to a private company *for operation.* The bill, as passed, was amended providing for a popular referendum on the question. In the elections of that year municipal ownership of rapid transits was approved by an overwhelming majority, the vote being 132,646 for and 42,916 against.

The commission made plans for the construction of the Manhattan and Bronx subways. The courts did not like these plans. They were "revised."

The city had a great deal of trouble in overcoming the constitutional limitation on its borrowing capacity. At that time, and even now, the city was head over heels in debt. The margin of credit appeared to be less than the estimated cost of construction, which ranged between $39,000,000 and $50,000,000. The money problem was partly solved by the successful consolidation on January 1, 1898, into one city of Greater New York, four counties and part of a fifth, four cities, twenty-one towns and fifteen villages, all of which, though having debts to be paid, had a combined borrowing capacity for greater than that of Manhattan alone. Then the adoption a year later of the constitutional amendments excepting certain county debts from the 10 per cent. limitation of the city's borrowing capacity widened the margin of credit still further.

When the city had money to spend, it soon discovered that it had many friends ready to do business with it. Accordingly, on February 21, 1900, what is known as Contract No. 1 was executed between the city and John B. MacDonald, who later assigned his contract to the Interborough Rapid Transit Company. Briefly, the agreement includes the following points:

1. The contractor, Mr. MacDonald, and his successor, the Interborough Rapid Transit Company, were required to build the subways and lay the tracks at the city's expense; the equipment to be provided by the contractor at his own expense.

2. The contractor is to operate the road for 50 years, with the right of renewal for 25 years more. During this period of 50 years the city is to receive annually the sum equal to the interest payable by the city upon the bonds it issued for the purpose of raising money for subway construction and also an annual sum of 1 per cent. of the entire amount so invested to be deposited in a fund, which at the end of the 50 years will be sufficient to retire all the bonds. If the company availed itself of its privilege to renew the lease for another 25 years it was required to pay

an annual rental not less than the average amount annually paid during the preceding 10 years.

3. At the end of the stipulated term the city was required to buy from the companies its rolling stock and other equipment in connection with the subways, at a reasonable price; in case of disagreement, the price to be fixed by arbitration.

4. The equipment, the property of the contractor as well as the subway itself were exempt from taxation. The fare was to be five cents. The general relation between the city and the company was that of landlord and tenant.

Contract No. 2, executed July 21, 1902, between the city and the Rapid Transit Subway Construction Company, which, on August 10, 1905, assigned its contract to the Interborough Rapid Transit Company, is substantially the same as Contract No. 1, except that the term of the lease is 35 years instead of 50 years. It also carries the privilege of renewal for 25 years. The 35-year provision was a concession to the protesting public against the injustice of the former contract. This subway was an extension from City Hall, Manhattan, to Atlantic Avenue, Brooklyn.

These are no contracts, they are holdups. The

city builds the subways, spends tens of millions of dollars of the people's money and gives them away free for fifty years to a corporation to make unheard-of profits on them.

This species of municipal ownership, so neatly "put over" on the people, ought to serve as a lesson, and it should be a warning to the honest advocates and adherents of collective ownership not to make alliances with, or place faith in politicans ever ready to exploit a popular demand, to use a healthy and sound principle as a vote-getter, and then pervert it to an evil use. Alluring promises in politics should be linked in with the general actions, economic and social beliefs as well as the past performances of those who make the promises.

The whole contract is camouflaged by the fact that at the end of 50 years the city will get the subways unencumbered. But who is removing the encumbrance? Did not the city pay for the construction of the subways? And is not the public paying the interest on bonds and building a retiring fund out of the fares it pays? What contribution is the Interborough making to this? None.

It is obvious that the company's allowance of

interest and sinking fund to the city is no payment at all for the privilege it has received. For had the company borrowed money on its own credit for the purpose of constructing subways, the principal and interest would have had to be paid in the course of 50 years, just as other bonds issued by the company. Such interests and sinking funds are fixed charges. They are taken out of the fares of the traveling public and are considered part of necessary expenses.

In a word, the lines are a pure gift to the Interborough.

To call these funds paid to the city "rentals" is to add insult to injury. By no stretch of the imagination can one truthfully call them a rental. As a matter of fact, what really happened was this: the city lent its credit to a private corporation whereby the corporation secured money not to exceed $50,000,000 on bonds bearing 3½ per cent. interest instead of 5 or 6 per cent., as might have been the case if the company itself, with its inferior credit, had to borrow it. Consequently, it is not the city that is getting any rentals, but the Interborough Rapid Transit Company. In the course of 50 years the company will receive from the city on this item alone somewhere between

$26,000,000 to $47,000,000. Not only does the company receive the franchise free, but it also receives an enormous subsidy into the bargain.

As might have easily been foreseen, the subways proved to be a gold mine. The company is earning up to this very day close to $7,000,000 profit annually, over and above all the excessive rentals, such as the one paid to the Manhattan Rilway Company for the elevated lines, all the "fixed charges," and all the interest on bonds. Eliminating unnecessary and swelled "charges" the company is earning between 20 and 25 per cent. profit on its actual investment. The city, which built the subways, earns nothing. It donated its right and property to a private corporation.

The returning of the roads to the city with the provision requiring it to buy the equipments of the company is not very alluring. With the rapid changes in the art of transportation and the rapid shifting of centers of population the old subways may either enjoy the standing of the present horse-car system or they may be so out of range of the traveling public as to become practically valueless.

CHAPTER IX

THE NOTORIOUS PARTNERSHIP

SUBWAY CONTRACTS OF 1913

Any problem not settled right is not settled at all. When the first subway projects were being planned, the legal limitations of the city's credit prevented the system from being comprehensive. The only two boroughs that were covered, and those not adequately, were Manhattan and the Bronx. Brooklyn was barely touched at all. Greater New York could hardly be satisfied with existing subways.

Meanwhile, the meaning of the first and second contracts was beginning to dawn upon the people. Its details were learned with great astonishment. It became clear that the city's interest had been bartered away. A hue and cry went up against any further dealings of that character. A wave of indignation swept the city. The agitation became so persistent that in 1906 a law was enacted forbidding the leasing of any new subways for longer than 25 years.

In 1907 the Board of Rapid Transit Commissioners were succeeded by the Public Service

Commission. This body was to be appointed by the Governor and was endowed with sweeping powers. All franchises were to be granted and public utility contracts entered into by the Commission on behalf of the city. Such agreements would not be binding, however, upon the city until the Board of Estimate and Apportionment had approved them.

Generally the state government has been Republican, the city administration Democratic—Tammany. The commission was created by a Republican Governor, Mr. Hughes. At the time the city was enjoying a Tammany Mayor, Mr. McClellan. A Republican commission and Democratic Board of Estimate and Apportionment are not likely to get along very sweetly. The dual authority was responsible for a great deal of unnecessary delay in the attempted solution of our transportation problem. For political reasons each body sought to discredit the action of the other, with the result that the city was scandalously neglected.

For eight years subway negotiations went on. Plans were made and remade. Proposals acceptable to the Commission were rejected by the Board of Estimate and Apportionment, and *vice versa.* Attempted schemes were dragged into the courts on six different occasions to prevent their execution. Demagogues on both sides played on the people for all the problem was worth, and it was worth a great deal. Politicians were made great, were elevated to the acme of municipal power, then dropped from the heights and consigned to the army of political pygmies in oblivion. Reputations were easily made and as easily destroyed.

The stake was indeed stupendous. The Rapid Transit plans involved an expense of over $330,-000,000 and an enlargement of the rapid transit carrying capacity to 2,000,000,000 passengers per annum, which is over 300,000,000 passengers more than the total number carried in the year 1912 on all New York City local transit lines, including the surface street cars. Such a stake is worth fighting for. He who got tangled up in these millions was caught in a golden net.

The struggle came to an end when, on March 19, 1913, the Public Service Commission for the First District, on behalf of the city, with the consent of the Board of Estimate and Apportionment, entered into a contract with two companies, the Interborough Rapid Transit Company and the New York Municipal Railway Company, a subsidiary of the Brooklyn Rapid Transit Company.

Generally, it may be said, the Interborough Company was to operate in Manhattan and the Bronx and touch a small part of the business heart of Brooklyn and Queens, while the Brooklyn Rapid Transit Company was to operate in Brooklyn and Queens. The former is known as Contract No. 3, the latter Contract No. 4.

The city acts in a dual capacity in these contracts, but that is not the reason the Rapid Transit plan is called the dual system. On the one hand, the city acts as a partner to each of the companies, on the other as a landlord.

The city is a partner in contributing vast sums of money, in furnishing franchises, and placing all the power and prestige of the metropolis back of the Rapid Transit system, but it is not a partner in reaping the enormous benefits flowing from such a system. For all practical purposes the partnership ends where benefits begin.

Having a voice in the management of the business or making provision for an equal division of earnings is not in line with the politicians' conception of sound municipal policy. On these questions the city puts on the garb of landlord; the operating company being the tenant. When the subway employees were out on strike for human conditions, the city authorities, even if they had the willingness—a sin with which it would hardly be fair to charge them—had no right "as a partner" to act in the matter, excepting to exert pressure indirectly such as any municipal authority would be able to exert on a company operating a public utility.

The contract is voluminous and involved, covering 700 printed pages. It goes into extreme details settling all questions imaginable, but hardly touching the interest of the city. After reading it one feels it is a document showing that New York has made an "agreement with the devil and a covenant with hell." Every stray dollar of the city's money has been annexed by the diligent companies while the annexing was good.

Mr. Shonts warns the city that unless fares are raised the city will lose tens of millions of dollars. His well-known friendship for the city is only excelled by his desire to get an 8-cent fare. Mr. Shonts perhaps remembers the arguments made against the notorious dual contract. It was then pointed out that the city will be a heavy loser; that accounts could be so manipulated by the company that even payment on interest and sinking fund on the city's investments would become impossible; that these conditions would be held up before the inhabitants of the city as an urge to grant new concessions to the company making the citizens believe they are doing it for their city.

These arguments were made before the war showing that the present financial "embarrassments" are not due so much to war conditions as to the inherent weaknesses of the contract. The outrageous demands of the companies must be met by hurling into their face the contracts they managed to impose upon the city.

The contract provides that the earnings of the old and new lines be pooled. It will be recalled that the old subways, built with city money, about $60,000,000 in all, net the city an amount equal to interest payable on the bonds issued for that purpose, a sum for a retiring fund *and no more.* This provision will continue until the end of the new contract.

The Interborough Rapid Transit Company, the operator with an actual investment of about $48,000,000, is to receive interest on the bonds issued, a sum for a retiring fund, plus $6,350,000 annually, representing its average annual net profit ending June 30, 1911. These $6,350,000 represent a little over 13 per cent. on the company's money invested, and is to be a guaranteed profit for a period of 50 years.

The companies made it certain that whatever changes are made in the local transit system, however unimportant the old subway lines may become, however little the old lines may actually earn because of having been superseded by other lines, the stupendous profits made in the early years of exceptional congestion and extreme neglect of property, should be guaranteed for its entire life. In other words, $317,500,000, almost seven times the investment proper, will be taken out of the earnings of the general rapid transit system, between 1915 and 1965 and given to the company as pure profit in payment for the successful robberies embodied in the contracts of 1900 and 1902.

It should be remembered further that the original contracts were to expire in 1954 and 1943, respectively, with the privilege of renewal for 25 years. The new contract makes all subway leases coterminus. It "levels" them up instead of down. It makes a bad bargain worse. It extends their terms considerably, making them last till December 31, 1965, and guarantees an annual preferential profit of $6,350,000 up to that date. This stupendous sum is to be paid before the city gets anything at all on its new investment; even before it receives interest on the bonds it issued for that purpose.

Although the city is an "equal partner," the company receives 6 per cent. on all the money it invests as a prior charge on earnings. When the company is all fed and satisfied the city gets the crumbs, if there are any. After all the company's "fixed charges" and huge preferentials have been paid, *if there is any money left*, the city is to get an equal share with that of the company on the money it furnished for the new lines. After the different funds have been paid and the various preferentials have been paid, including the city's share, if there is still any money left, it is to be divided equally between the company and the city. Only supreme optimists should expect these divisible profits to come true. It is to be remembered that the lines and their finances are administered by the companies, in whose interest it is to manipulate it so that there will be no profit apparent. And so it has worked out.

Under this agreement the company can easily swell the cost of operation, thereby precluding any possible revenue to the city; not even the interest on its bonds. Although the city is given the right to challenge any item of expense, that is no guarantee against abuse, because a company powerful enough to make the city officials enter into such objectionable and unbeneficial contracts can easily silence other officials when silence is necessary.

An instance, although in itself small, will illustrate how expenses can be manipulated. About three months prior to the signing of the contract, when it was fairly certain that it would be signed, the salary of President Shonts was raised from $50,000 to $100,000 per annum, and the salary of Vice-President Hedley from $25,000 to $40,000 per annum. The salaries were almost doubled, and yet, by reason of the new arrangement, the company did not lose anything thereby; on the contrary, it gained $5,000. Formerly the company spent $75,000 on the salaries of its president and vice-president. Now, with the city as partner, though the salaries were almost doubled, it pays only $70,000. By extending this method into all departments, the corporation can pile up a deficit on the city, then stoutly claim to be its warmest friend and demand higher fares in the interest of the city itself.

The unsatisfied longings and forlorn hopes of the corporations in the past 20 years were answered fully in the contracts of 1913. For years the elevated railroad company tried hard to third-track their lines. This was denied by different administrations for different reasons. The day when the companies got what they wanted for a minimum consideration (to the city) came. The agreement gives the Interborough and the Brooklyn Rapid Transit Companies the right to rebuild the old elevated lines wherever necessary and to third-track them.

The new franchise for third-tracking is given for 85 years and is indeterminate after the first 10 years. There is no compensation to the city for these franchises. The Chicago plan, which is by no means to be held out as a model, at least compelled the companies to yield their perpetual franchises before the agreement was entered into in 1907.

New York, with the experience of Chicago to go by, with the experience of Cleveland, which settled its transportation problem in 1907, with the experience of every European city to learn from, did not even secure this concession from the companies. The policy of the city seemed to be: A maximum of the city's rights for a minimum consideration.

There is another point in the contract bearing directly on the demand of fares. It is so strikingly unjust to the people that its acceptance by the city must have surpassed the fondest dreams of the corporations. That is true of both contracts, the New York and the Brooklyn. The enormous expense involved in the reconstruction and improvement of existing elevated railroads is charged entirely to capital account, fully amortized within a period of 50 years, although the companies' franchises are for 85 years.

In other words, the fare-payers pay all costs, all the expenses, establish a fund to maintain the roads at the top-notch of efficiency, create an amortization fund which in 50 years will be large enough to buy out the entire reconstruction project, then had it over to the companies in perpetual possession. The public will cheerfully pay for the operation and maintenance of the road but it refuses, or rather should refuse, to buy a road for the company. The company blows hot and cold at the same time. It wants the fare-payers to buy an elevated railroad for it, at the same time it demands huge profits now, immediately.

The New York *Sun* says the only way "to convert the average loss on every passenger carried," —which is not true, by the way, as there is no average loss—"into an average gain" is to raise the fares. Even if there were an average loss there is a far better way of converting it into an average gain. Let all the unnecessary charges against the fare-payers be removed and the gain will be substantial. The 1913 contract fixes the fare at five cents. If the *Sun* believes the contract ought to be changed, it will be strongly supported. But the changes in the contract must not increase the burdens of the public. Advantage should be taken of this opportunity to release the city from the grip of the corporations.

It is to be remembered that the agreement is not over-generous to the public in its fare provisions. While the Interborough Rapid Transit Company owns both systems, the subway and the elevated lines, two separate fares are charged, with no system of transfers, excepting at one unimportant point. In this respect again we are behind other cities. Where transportation contracts are so general, as the one concluded in 1913, the one-city-one-fare principle has been established.

The company takes no risk at all in this "partnership." Should the city find at some later date that certain extensions are necessary they will be built on the same "partnership basis." But if there is a deficit in the enterprise the city is to sustain it.

A great deal has been said about the recapture clause in the contract. The city's right to recapture the new lines after the first ten years is an absurdity; while sounding excellently on paper in practice it is an impossibility. The new lines are intertwined inseparably with the old ones. The old lines cannot be recaptured. Of what value will the recapture of part of the system be? Each line will charge a separate fare. Little enthusiasm could be worked up for a municipal ownership that increases fares and inconveniences. The companies were fully aware of this practical difficulty when they consented to the "recapture" clause.

It is the usual method in modern contracts between corporations and a city to have a few alluring and apparently beneficial provisions as a sop to the "mob," then to vitiate their beneficial effects by the insertion of some insurmountable practical obstacle.

The people are demanding formal promises rather than substantial relief. This is easily granted. The 1913 contract was supposed to have been a great compromise by inserting a clause giving the city the empty right to recapture the lines after the first ten years. The people were satisfied, the politicians chuckled, and the corporations got away with it.

CHAPTER X

"DEAD CAPITAL" EARNING MONEY

John Smith establishes a $2,000,000 business. John Smith is very greedy. He does not insure his business against fire. Insurance costs money. It is a charge against earnings, generally considered a legitimate and necessary charge. But he wants to pocket all the earnings, which, by reason of a certain monopoly he enjoys, are substantial, $200,000 per annum. Ten per cent. is considered a fair rate of profit and Smith is satisfied.

A fire occurs. Smith's business is half destroyed. He rebuilds it, placing it on the same footing as before. This costs $1,000,000. Smith figures his investment now $3,000,000.

The business earns the usual $200,000. This time the rate of profit, according to the new capitalization, is not very large—6.66 per cent.

Smith refuses to profit by his experience. He fails to take those elementary precautions for the safety of his property which are considered indispensable by prudent business men. He again declines to insure the business against fire. Now there is an additional excuse for his action, his rate of profit is low.

In the course of a few years another fire occurs, more damaging than before. It practically destroys the entire plant. Unwilling to abandon his valuable monopoly, his special privilege, Smith sets out to rebuild his business. This time it costs $2,000,000. According to Smith, his investment is now $5,000,000.

The business earns the usual $200,000 a year. The rate of interest, however, according to the new capitalization is decidedly low, only 4 per cent.

Smith raises a howl. He cannot afford to sell his product as "cheap" as he did before; for he is losing money. A business earning only 4 per cent. profit on actual investment is a losing proposition. And Smith can prove with his books that he has actually invested $5,000,000.

Is there a sane person who would say Smith is entitled to a raise in the price of his product? Who is there so naive as to contend that the public should compensate Smith for his ignorance and greed? If there be such a person he should be told that underneath the ashes of the "burnt capital" there lies a $2,000,000 business still earning the high rate of profit of 10 per cent. and Smith should have no complaint.

The railroad companies are in the position of Smith. They built their roads in the fifties and sixties, some of them earlier than that. By reason of the revolutionary changes in the arts, transportation machinery changed decade by decade. Motive power alone has undergone three complete changes—animal, cable and electric. The nature of the cars and equipment had passed through many metamorphoses and there are still, no doubt, many it will pass in time to come.

When the horse-car lines became obsolete and had to be abandoned, and cable roads established in their place, the companies simply issued new bonds or stock, as the case happened to be, to finance the change. The capitalization of the road, assuming no inflated issues, was the original cost of the horse-car lines, plus the additional money required to rebuild the lines into cable roads. When cars were badly worn, dilapidated and useless, the company bought new cars. It raised money for that purpose by issuing new stocks and bonds, thus adding more book value to the properties.

When the cable roads became out of date and the lines were to be electrified, the companies again issued stocks and bonds to meet the expenses.

This time the outlay was enormous because the cost of electric lines was comparatively high. Along with the change of motive power there are what may be termed incidental changes in cars, equipment, etc. The expenses to accomplish these changes were always met by the issuance of new stocks and bonds.

The net result of all this is a book capitalization of the railroad properties far out of proportion to their actual physical value.

It is obvious that when the people used a cable road they did not get more service out of it just because it was built on the grave of a horse-car line. When the traveler used a cable road he did not at the same time use a horse-car line. They should not, therefore, be expected to pay profits on two roads.

Similarly, when people travel in an electric car they do not get more service out of it because it is founded on the outlived cable road. They surely do not get more service out of an electric line built on a street where a cable road operated formerly than they would if it were an original line built entirely new. Why, then, expect of them a fare that will suffice to pay interest and profits on the new capital, as well as the capital that had been invested on roads that have long ceased to exist?

Yet the rate of fare has always been determined on precisely such basis. *And the demand now being made to raise fares is largely because the fare-payer is expected to pay interest and profits, not only on investments in lines upon which he travels, but also on investments on lines that have long ceased to exist.*

Capital that was invested in the now dead and useless lines is *dead capital;* and dead capital cannot earn money.

To reserve a sufficient portion of the revenue to replace capital consumed during the year, but not requiring replacement within the year, is a primary requisite and a conservative business principle. Such a replacement fund is considered part of the capital itself. To divide the entire annual surplus among the stockholders without first establishing a proper replacement fund is equivalent to stealing a given sum annually from the capital itself and dividing it among the stockholders. Put that way, it is clear that the companies have been committing a criminal offense; hidden under a maze of business detail, the companies' practices are excused on the ground of "mistaken business judgment," etc.

If the companies, in violation of every business principle, following a policy of "get rich quick," were too greedy to diminish their fat earnings by laying aside annually a fund for the purpose of meeting such obvious expenses as replacement of old, worn out, dilapidated and obsolete roads, and cost of equipment, should the people be taxed to compensate them for their greed?

The companies knew that after a few years the old roads would have to be scrapped and replaced by new ones. They knew, as a matter of certainty, that things used fall into disrepair. Why did they not prepare to meet these necessities, as prudent business men should?

The case of Smith is less sinful. He gambled. There was as much chance for his business to escape the ravages of fire as not. But the railway companies knew that the destruction of their property was not a matter of accident but a matter of use and time. Yet they delibertely refused to insure their property by failing to establish an adequate replacement fund.

Moreover, the profits of the companies in the early days were fabulous. During the period of horse-car operation the Third Avenue Company paid at one time as high as 25 per cent. dividends, the average being about 13 per cent.

During the operation of the cable roads, there was already the dead weight of the horse-car lines attached to the new capitalization. Yet the earnings still appeared large. It is estimated by the Public Service Commission that "the company could have amortized or accumulated by sinking fund a sufficient amount to have paid off the entire cost of the road as set forth above, *and still have paid dividends of over 8 per cent.** and founded a reserve fund besides."†

When the Third Avenue Company reorganized, after its lines were in the hands of a receiver for over three years, it insisted upon capitalizing the dead roads. It issued securities for millions of dollars over and above the actual physical value of the property on the ground that the books showed that its constituent members, also in the hands of receivers, had invested that money in lines now extinct. This they did contrary to the commission's warnings that the securities "far ex-

* Italics are mine.

† Third Avenue R. R. Co. Case No. 1181, 2 P. S. C. Reports, p. 347.

ceeded the value of the property and that the evidence as to net income did not indicate that interest and dividends would be *earned* upon the securities proposed."*

"The statement is made as to the Third Avenue Railroad Company proper, that in the present book cost of road and equipment and in the liabilities which are outstanding, there is an amount about $2,000,000 for horse-car lines and equipment and about $8,000,000 for cable roads. These figures have not been proved, but whatever may be the amounts, the question is whether the new company should be allowed to issue securities that do not represent any property acquired or necessary expenses connected with such property."†

The capitalizing of "dead capital" so definitely established in the Third Avenue System is not without its examples in other companies. Among the colleagues of the Third Avenue company, indulging to excess in this vicious and deceptive practice, is the New York Railways system, now in the hands of a receiver, where it logically belongs.

---

* Third Avenue R. R. Co. Case No. 1181, 3 P. S. C. Reports, p. 21.

† Third Avenue Co. Case 1181, 2 P. S. C. Reports, p. 347.

It should be noted that these two companies between them control practically all the surface lines in Manhattan and the Bronx, as well as much of Westchester county.

The New York Railways Company is the successor of the defunct Metropolitan Street Railway Company. Upon the latter's reorganization, the Public Service Commission, in analyzing the securities about to be issued by the applicant's reorganization committee, said:

"*The applicants submitted an estimate of property that had ceased to exist, amounting to over* $13,355,000, *apportioned as follows:**

Horse-car system	$6,640,439
Cable system	5,371,698
Compressed air equipment.........	386,794
Storage battery equipment.........	956,714

"The first item does not include all of the horse-car lines, only those that have disappeared entirely.

"*It is unnecessary to discuss the accuracy of these estimates, for it is admitted that the property does not exist; . . .*"*†

---

* Italics are mine.

† Re: Metropolitan Railway Company reorganization case 1305, 3 P. S. C. Reports, p. 113.

Do the companies expect the "dead capital" to earn dividends? Shall the people pay on an investment that does not exist? It may be of interest to have the companies explain whether these false capitalizations have anything to do with the present financial failures.

About half of the capitalization of old roads consists of "dead capital" and investments never made. The companies insist that the people should be compelled to pay a fare high enough to pay dividends on this false capitalization.

CHAPTER XI

PUNISHING THE PUBLIC FOR ITS TOLERANCE

AMORTIZATION THE MEANS

During the great financial crash of 1907 almost all surface railway companies in New York went into the hands of receivers. When the atmosphere cleared, committees of bondholders for the benefit of whom the courts were administering the various properties, got together and decided to reorganize the business and set them up on a normal basis. They submitted their contemplated reorganization plans to the Public Service Commission, then young and inclined to be useful.

The reorganized companies assumed all bonded indebtedness contracted in 20 years of reckless and criminal gambling. Prior to the collapse the railway companies were wild with speculation. The rails of the street cars were worth their weight in gold, as far as the debt and the interest it carried with it were concerned.

"The funded debt of all the leased roads, apart from the Metropolitan Street Railway," reports the Public Service Commission, "was increased from $11,000,000 to $62,000,000. The bonded debt of the Metropolitan Street Railway Company was increased from $9,000,000 in 1897 to $44,000,000 in 1907, although this company has but twenty-eight miles of electric tracks, *so that the bonded debt per mile of electric track was* $1,500,000, *nearly twice the cost per mile of track of constructing and equipping the present subway.** In view of the condition existing it is not surprising that the system broke down and that receivers were appointed to take charge of various companies."†

Upon a careful inquiry of the proposed securities to be issued by the reorganized companies and a liberal appraisal of the properties by experts, the Commission decided that the amount of securities proposed to be issued was far out of proportion to the real value of the property.

In the Third Avenue system the total securities proposed to be issued amounted to $73,623,744.32, while the physical value and assets of all the companies included in the reorganization scheme, liberally estimated, amounted to no more than $44,046,637.72. The excesses of securities

* Italics are mine.

† P. S. C. Reports, First District, 1909, p. 25.

issued over the fair value of the property was nearly $30,000,000. Naturally, the Commission declined to permit the company to carry out its plan. Upon an appeal to the court the company secured a decision denying the Commission the right to limit the amount of securities to be issued by a reorganized company, even if the issue has no relation to the actual physical value of the property.

A similar course was taken by the New York Railways Company. The total amount of securities it issued was $104,930,500 against properties liberally estimated to be worth no more than $85,801,000. The excess of securities over liabilities here was $19,129,500, based upon the most liberal estimates.

Having been directed by the courts to grant the applicants' request, the Commission turned from the futile and thankless task of defending the interests of the people to the more appreciative work of serving the property interests, the investing bankers, the insurance companies. In upper circles there was universal approval of the Commission's action. At last it had found its proper sphere of activity and discovered its purpose for existence.

At all expense, business must be made safe and sound—became the policy of the Commission. Securities once issued, whether they represent any property or not, should be amortized fully.

Business should pay for itself. The aim of the science of modern finance is to make industry self-sustaining and devoid of risk. Public utilities are most amenable to such scientific financing because of their being subject to regulation by government bodies. Rates are raised and in some cases lowered, depending on the ability of the utility to pay interest on its bonded indebtedness, maintain the various reserve funds, and pay a "fair" dividend.

Should it appear that a public utility corporation, conducting itself in accordance with the Commission's prescribed rules of accountancy, doe not earn sufficient to show "fair" return on its investments, rates will be raised by the government and the people have no option but to pay as told.

This is the situation to-day in the local railroad fare controversy.

Amortization, a sound business principle in itself, is now invoked by special privilege to shield its criminal work just as other sciences are often employed for vicious ends.

The principle of amortization is simple enough.

The management of the roads is to lay aside annually from earnings sufficient sums, separately kept, to provide for (1) depreciation, wear and tear and absolescence; (2) the redeeming of bonds when due; (3) general reserve; (4) interest on bonds; (5) guaranteed dividends.

These are prime requisites. A corporation that cannot meet these obligations is bankrupt. The various sums requisite for each fund are determined by experts in the employ of the Commission.

The first fund is created to maintain the roads in first-class condition, to insure good and efficient service. It is also to be used for the purpose of meeting the ever-changing development in the arts, the introduction of new motive power, the replacement of wooden cars by steel cars, etc. That is the theory.

The second fund is to be used for the purpose of retiring the bonds issued to raise money to defray the first cost of construction, the building and equipping of the roads. By means of this fund the business buys itself out in a stated period of time.

The other funds are self-explanatory.

There can be no objection to this principle of finance under the present business system, except when it is misapplied. The manner in which amortization has been practiced on the New York public is outrageous.

To grasp fully the meaning of this in its relation to the demand for higher fares, to appreciate the effrontery of the traction trust, and its unsound claims, it is necessary to examine briefly two questions.

1. What is being amortized?

2. The railroads and equipments having been fully amortized, paid for, who comes into possession of them?

In the first place, the investment in the surface railway systems amounting close to $300,000,000, is to be amortized fully out of the fare payers' pockets within a period of about fifty years. The same government body prescribing the rule for amortization of bonds will also see to it that a fund is created to maintain the lines at top-notch efficiency. At the end of the fifty years or so, the private companies will come into possession of the street railway systems, all paid for.

If the public is made to pay for roads, upon what principle should the companies come into possession of them? It is not clear upon what theory the government bases such policy, except possibly on the theory that it is the divine right of corporations to sit on the backs of the people forever.

The third-tracking of the elevated lines is another case of giving something for nothing. The people amortize the cost of this expensive project within fifty years only to give the lines to the companies entirely unencumbered. This case has already been more fully discussed under the head of "The Notorious Partnerships."

If the tax annually placed upon the people for the purpose of buying property, by way of amortization, for private corporations is unjust and burdensome, the amortization of all the accumulated "dead capital," watered-stock and over-capitalization generally, is outrageous. And acutally to demand higher fares for this purpose is, to put it mildly, highway robbery.

The largest single item in the over-capitalization of the New York Railways Company's reorganization scheme, it will be remembered, was "dead capital" amounting at the very least to $13,335,645. Speaking of the class of securities that must be amortized under its rules, the Commission said: "The mere statement of the problem indicates that *property which does not exist must be included in that class.** If securities have been issued for such properties to the extent of $13,335,000, they certainly belong in the class to be amortized."

But who pockets all these vast sums of money that are being collected from the daily users of our transit lines under the guise of "amortization"? Who are these high lords to whom large feudal fees must be paid submissively and without a protest? Who are these figures dimly seen moving behind the curtains and wielding such a tremendous power over organized government, the press, and even the people?

They are not the small stockholders. They are not the petty investors. They are the princes of high finance, in whose presence, we, the humble people, stand with bared heads and trembling souls gladly offering our all.

Investing bankers and insurance companies, generally, supply the money to the railroad companies. The bonds that are issued appear to bear 3½, 4 or 5 per cent. interest. One should not fall into the error of believing that this interest is all

---

* Italics are mine.

the financiers get. There are more subtle ways of receiving a usurious interest. The bankers seldom pay for bonds more than the actual physical value of property represented by them, regardless of their indicated value. When the time of redeeming the bonds arrives, however, the investors receive not what they paid for the certificates, but what their face value indicates.

Thus, when the Third Avenue Railroad Company offered its bond issue, according to the bondholder's committee's own statement, one class of bonds amounting to $15,790,000, was selling at about 80, another class of bonds to the amount of $22,536,000 was selling at about 70, while the $16,590,000 of stock was selling at 30. In other words, the banker pays $70 for a bond, draws 5 per cent. interest on $100 annually, for 50 years, and in 1960 he returns the bond to the company receiving for it full value of $100. The fare-payer, therefore, pays to the banker, through a middle-man, the railroad company, a 5 per cent. interest for 50 years on $100, when only $70 was borrowed, plus a special bonus of $30 upon the bonds' redemption.

Heretofore this bonus was not as secured as it is to-day, under government control. Now the government sees to it that the public puts aside enough money annually to amortize the bond at par, even though it was sold at 70.

The total difference between the par value of the securities issued in the Third Avenue System and the actual value paid for them by the financiers is approximately $25,000,000. This has gone to the bankers.

In the New York Railways system $104,930,-500 bonds were marketed on a similar basis. Even so rich a company as the Interborough, when marketing its bonds allows a large bonus to the bankers.

The net result of this is that the fare-payers are obliged to pay interest on tens of millions of dollars on money never borrowed, and also to amortize this gigantic sum to be paid to the financiers as a bonus when the bonds are redeemed. If a five-cent fare is not sufficient for all this an eight-cent fare will cover it.

It is significant that the government, which is supposed to stand guard over the people's interest, is directly instrumental, through the Public Service Commission, in collecting this money for the bankers and other investing interests.

The amortization of many millions of dollars

which were never invested is a new, scientific and legal way of picking the people's pockets.

The Railroad Securities Commission in its report to the President of the United States strongly urged that "no limitation should be placed on the price at which bonds can be sold, but any discount should be cancelled or amortized during the life of the bonds by the apportion each year out of annual income or surplus accumulated after the issue of the bonds of any less than the proportionate amount of the discount."*

The Public Service Commission agreed with the Securities Commission entirely.

"It has been the invariable practice of the Commission to require the difference between the cash proceeds of the bonds and their par value to be treated the same as bank discount or interest paid in advance and to be amortized within the term of the obligation."

And it adds: "the propriety of this requirement has never been contested by any of the corporations affected."†

Why should the corporations object? They

* P. S. C. Reports, v. 3, p. 55.
† P. S. C. Reports, v. 3, p. 56.

lose nothing by it; on the contrary, they gain a great deal. The people, and not they, pay.

When "no limitation" is placed on the price at which bonds can be sold, the financiers, through their bankers, buy bonds from their vassals, the railroad corporations, for a next-to-nothing price fully assured by the government that the bonds will be redeemed, at par, with moneys collected from the people, in annual installments, after a stated term of years.

In the reorganization proceedings of the New York Railways system there appears an item of $4,740,000 under the head of "Franchise Payments" against which securities were issued. This item is of extraordinary interest, not because of its amount, but as an illustration of the effrontery of the companies. Chapter VII deals with the methods employed by the companies in securing franchises.

The companies stop at nothing. All means, fair and foul, are employed. If money has been spent, it has not been spent in paying the city for franchises, but in bribing the Aldermen and corrupting the government. The Public Service Commission says that "Although a careful inquiry was made, neither the applicants nor the experts of the commission have been able to find that any company existing, whose lines are now operated as a part of the system under discussion, has ever paid the city anything for franchise rights, except in two instances, totalling $150,000."*

There is only one theory upon which the company can justify the capitalization of franchises at $4,740,000, for which only $150,000 were paid to the city. The people being too timid to demand a return of the stolen goods ought, in justice, be punished by making them pay all expenses incurred in securing the theft, plus compound interest. And the penalty is inflicted with a vengeance. Not only is the traveling public to pay interest for the next 50 years on securities issued against these "Franchise Payments," but also have it amortized, so that, in 1960, somebody will get $4,740,000, easy money.

This generation is hard hit, as far as transportation goes, for still another reason. The building of the new subways involved a tremendous layout.

When the new subway contracts were being planned, the city was in no financial condition to build them itself or be an equal partner. Its total

---

* Re: Metropolitan Street Railway, reorganization, 3, P. S. C. Reports, p. 113.

debt was so huge that the constitutional limitation upon its borrowing capacity left a very narrow margin for further loans.

The propertied classes, whose voices are usually heard in legislative halls, and who are the determining factor in matters of public expense, found themselves between the devil and the deep sea. They were torn between two conflicting interests.

A better system of transportation means a greater and more prosperous city. It means the rise in the value of real estate and higher rents. It means fat contracts for the construction companies, high interest to the investors, fat underwriting fees to the bankers, and large fees to promoters. In a word, it means prosperity to the money class. On the other hand, to issue municipal bonds for subway purposes may mean higher taxes with which to pay interest, and build a sinking fund for those bonds. There is little choice in such an embarrassing situation.

It was finally agreed that the constitution be amended to increase the city's power to incur indebtedness for such public utilities as should prove self-supporting or profitable, as such debts would impose no burden on the taxpayer.

The burden was shifted entirely from the taxpayer to the fare-payer, the public. Between the two the taxpayer wins, almost always.

According to this constitutional amendment in which Governor Hughes, the Public Service Commission and most "civic bodies" concurred, the bonds issued for subway construction have to be fully amortized out of earnings, in order that this debt be considered one incurred in a self-supporting industry. Interests on these bonds and all other charges, must be paid out of the same source and for the same reason.

The contract between the city and the companies, therefore, provides that all bonds be amortized within 50 years, interest paid and every necessary expense borne by the traveling public. The fare must be large enough to cover all these charges; if it is not, the authorities can be dependent upon to see to it that it is. The companies' investment is to be amortized within these 50 years, besides.

The people are being humored into believing that they are getting subway systems and equipments free in 1965. The fact is they are to pay for the subways and equipment out of their fares. The company loses nothing.

Of course, the amortization of so gigantic a

sum as the 1913 contracts involve when added to the various unnecessary guaranteed profits in the form of rentals and just plain profits in the form of dividends, makes the burden upon the public exceptionally heavy.

The fact is deliberately overlooked that the property holders of the city, not only as part of the general public, but as property holders, derive a special benefit from the Rapid Transit facilities. The cost of first construction should not, therefore, fall entirely on the fare-payers.

If the amortization of the costs of the subways exclusively out of earnings, under the present partnership is objectionable, if the amortization of the third-tracking project on the elevated lines and the actual physical value of the street railways systems is unjust to the public, the amortization of the watered-stock, "dead capital" and over-capitalization generally, exclusively out of earnings, is outrageous.

There is but one excuse for making the people amortize everything in sight, that is, to save a tottering system. Gambling, speculation, appropriation of earnings that should have gone to maintain the business, criminal mismanagement—all these have brought the traction systems to ruin. The collapse was inevitable. Something had to be done to save the decayed system of private ownership. The business had to be rehabilitated, placed on a solid footing again.

The Government, therefore, created a Public Service Commission. The courts hemmed and hedged in its power so that it might not wander into strange gardens and untrod paths. The Commission caught the "spirit in the air." It proceeded to crystallize all the speculations, all the insane economic adventures, all the vices of an irrational system of private ownership of public utilities into funds to be amortized, paid for by the people, in installments, under the Commission's own gentle guidance.

This is what may rightly be called capitalism guaranteed by the government.

CHAPTER XII

THE BANKRUPTCY OF REGULATION

For a long time past two principles proposing to offer relief from the unspeakable abuses of private ownership of public utilities have been battling for supremacy. One principle is that of public ownership and operation; the other is that of private ownership, subject to public regulation.

Each principle has enlisted for its support a great mass of people of varied political opinions and of various degrees of advocacy.

Both movements have conceded that something must be done. Things could not go on as they were. The constantly growing evil was too great and too menacing to permit of indifference.

The collectivists, as the believers in public ownership are called, range from the out-and-out Socialists, who believe that all socially necessary industries should be collectively owned and demomratically managed, to the mere municipal ownership reformers, who hold that only what can be conservatively defined as public utilities—such as water supply, gas plants, railways and the like—

should be owned by the Government, while the rest of the industries can best be taken care of by private ownership and management.

The regulationists, likewise, are of varied degree. They differ on what should be subject to regulation and on the extent to which the policy of government interference in private affairs should be permitted.

The principle of regulation won. It won because it received support from all sorts of elements. It made its appeal to that portion of the population which honestly believe that the evils of private ownership can be alleviated and social progress best served by constant governmental guidance and watch over the wicked corporations and the frailties of human nature. It made its appeal to the great mass of frightened mediocrity who saw in collective ownership the advent of the horrible "red." It made its appeal to the cunning apologists of special interests who saw in regulation a means of diverting popular attention and preserving the present system.

Though carrying the day and in possession of full power to follow their ideas, the regulationists soon realized the hollowness of their victory. To be in possession of power is not sufficient. It is more important to so use that power as to insure its retention.

This they could not do because they were not certain of their ground. They chose to attach strings and limitations to their triumph. There was a feeling that their solution was temporary and insufficient. It could not stand the test of time.

The theory of regulation, briefly put, is this: Public utilities are indispensable public needs. Their private ownership and control results in certain abuses and evils. Private owners cannot be relied upon to serve the public disinterestedly. Stipulations in contracts or in franchise grants are no guarantee that the safety and convenience of the public is assured, because what may be an ample safeguard at the time relations are entered into may prove a menace and a fetter years later. conditions of the community change and with altered conditions arise new and different requirements. A rigid contract is entirely inconsistent with the interests of an ever-changing and growing society.

Therefore, a group of wise and trustworthy men are to be appointed by the Governor, "by and with the advice and consent of the Senate," for a term of five years to be the direct agents of the public in its dealings with public utility corporations. These Commissioners should be experts in the extremely complex problems of public utilities. They are given sweeping power to hear, investigate and pass upon complaints against public utility corporations, to prescribe rules for the proper conduct of the business, and decide upon rates to be charged to the public.

The Commission is to be on guard constantly. With every change in the life and development of the community it is to prescribe such rules and regulations as to meet with its new needs and requirements.

It should be noted, incidently, that the theory of regulation is contrary to our system of government based, as it is, on the system of checks and balances. The Commission is the incarnation of all three functions, legislative, judicial and administrative. It is what may be designated as government by commission.

This inconsistency explains the many conflicts between the courts and the Commission in its early days. Regulation carried to its logical conclusion is decidedly out of harmony with the recognized rights of "vested interests."

If regulation is reared on a contradiction in theory, it is beset with insurmountable difficulties in practice.

A sincere desire to be good, to observe the rules of the game, and to demand that others be and do likewise, may be sound and lofty idealism, but it will not secure the ends sought, unless there is, side by side with good intentions, a practical program removing the material conditions which make it easier and more profitable for men to do evil than to do good.

The regulationists failed because they did not have a practical program. They did not base their theories upon fact. They did not take into account the interplay of political and economic interests under a system of private ownership. They did not recognize the fact that corporations control governors and legislatures and, therefore, they can easily control commissions, which are the mere appointees of these public officials. They did not comprehend that the more corporation interests will depend on the direct say-so of public agents, the more reason there is for the corporations to exert their almost irresistible power to secure governors and commissions who are subservient to their will.

Regulation in practice, therefore, not only fails to purify the economic lake, but aggravates the situation by polluting the political waters.

Although in a vague and indefinite way New York had regulatory bodies for many years past, the beginning of regulation in the modern sense in this city and state dates back to 1907.

The Public Service Commission, appointed under the complicated Public Service Commission's law, divides the state into two Districts. The First District operates in Greater New York; it represents the city in its dealings with the public utility corporations, except the railroads running out of the city, and the telephones and telegraphs. The salaries of the five commissioners, as originally organized, are $15,000 per annum; their secretary and counsel are paid by the state, while the rest of the expense is a mandatory charge on the municipality.

Governor Hughes, the sponsor of the commission idea in this state, recklessly trampled on every principle of municipal home rule in forcing the commission upon the city.

The Commission for the Second District operates in the rest of the state and covers telegraphs and telephones for the city, as well as those railroads that terminate in New York. As far as regulation is concerned both districts possess similar powers.

The people's experience with the Commission is sad and disappointing. The Commissioners' incompetence and unwillingness to represent the people exceeded the forecasts of the worst regulation opponents.

The Commissions have kow-towed to the corporations from the very beginning. Their members were either former employees of the corporations they were set to regulate or they enjoyed lively expectations and perhaps promises to be "picked off" when their arduous tasks as commissioners were over, or they were so incompetent and indifferent to their duties that their handling of their duty bordered on the grotesque. Occasionally a member of ability and character would find his way on the Commission. But he would be continually out-voted, and if he made too much noise he would be dropped.

When the Hon. John A. Dix, the Murphy Governor, had to fill a vacancy on the Commission, he appointed George V. S. Williams, a Brooklyn lawyer, who some years previously had been connected with the legal staff of the Brooklyn Rapid Transit Company. He, of course, showed healthy signs of appreciation of his former employers' interests and generally lined up on all questions on the side of the corporations. He was a strong supporter of the notorious 1913 contracts.

William R. Willcox, chairman of the New York Commission from the day of its creation to February 1, 1913, upon his retirement from duty, was "picked off" by the Hudson and Manhattan Railroad Company, a corporation Mr. Willcox was supposed to have been regulating for about six years, and he was made its counsel in a capitalization case before the Commission. The New York Edison Company, a subsidiary of the Consolidated Gas Company, also appreciated the value of having a former chairman of the Commission appear as its counsel before his former associates, and so it retained Mr. Willcox in a big rate case.

Frank W. Stevens was the chairman of the upstate Commission. His ability was soon recognized by the corporations appearing before him. No talent is too brilliant or too costly for the vested interests if it can only be purchased and enlisted in its defense. Before Mr. Stevens, upon being retired to private life, had time to shed a tear over his retirement, the New York Central Railroad Company retained him as its general counsel.

That the public utility corporations have been taking their attorneys preferably from among former commissioners is not to be wondered at. It is understood that they do not employ the commissioner, but the attorney; he having been well trained, of course, at public expense. If, when this attorney comes before the Commission in a rate or capitalization case, he adds to the weight of his legal talent his influence with his former associates and wins a point, it is his privilege. The corporations see in it a mere coincidence. Only evil minds will criticise such innocent transactions.

Again, who will forget the famous appointment to the chairmanship of the First District Commission of the Honorable Edward E. McCall, Tammany darling, chum of Murphy, and interested party in the Kings County Electric Light and Power Company, a powerful corporation in Brooklyn that he was set to regulate. As was later learned, this man was appointed by the honorable and valiant William Sulzer, the "People's Governor," at the behest of Murphy.

McCall as a regulator not only by reason of his personal interest in certain public utility corporations, but by general training and environment, typifies in his person the bankruptcy of the entire regulation policy.

The Public Service Commission became the football of politics. With every change of administration at Albany there has been an upheaval in the Commission. The Governor has the right to remove commissioners for cause. Invariably, the Governor has sufficient ground for removal if he so chose. When the statesmanly Dix became governor the Commission was investigated. When Whitman, Republican, presidential aspirant, reigned there was an investigation and some removals. Now, when Mr. Smith, Democrat, is in power the usual investigation is proposed.*

The net result of the twelve years of the Public Service Commission's life is a shameful surrender of the city's interests. A system of subways,

---

* Since this chapter was written the Commission for the First District has been reorganized. At the suggestion of the Governor, the Commission now consists of one. Lewis Nixon was appointed. He is spared the inconvenience of having minority reports. He is unanimous on all questions.

financed by the city, maintained and amortized by the public, has been tenderly handed over to private corporations by the Commission for a period of 50 years, to reap hundreds of million of dollars in profits. It bartered away the valuable right in the elevated third-tracking franchise without any consideration; and, moreover, it pledged the public to buy out the roads for the corporations. It has not reduced rates. It has not improved service commensurate with the expense and sacrifice the city has been making. It has not improved the safety of the traveling public. It has not improved the conditions of the workers employed on the lines. It has long ceased to regulate the corporations in the interest of the public and has very effectively regulated the public in the interest of the corporations. Its function has been reduced to guaranteeing and protecting corporation investments, proper or improper.

The Public Service Commission is one with the corporation according to a bill recently introduced by Assemblyman Martin of Oneida County, the purpose of which is the raising of fares to 7 or 8 cents. The Commission filed an extensive brief with the Legislative Committee to which the bill was referred, giving reason why the bill should become a law.

Instead of the corporation engaging highly paid counsel to argue and push its legislation, the Commission receiving its pay from the people does it ungrudgingly. Its services are so much more valuable to the corporations because the Commission is clothed with government authority. Its arguments and pleas are weightier than those of private counsel by reason of the mistaken view that it represents the people.

Here is another case where a reform, sponsored by a movement whose general purpose is to save the present system, ultimately becomes a weapon in the hands of the capitalist class.

The policy of regulations has failed, and failed badly.

One of the signs—if not conclusive, at least indicative—showing that regulation failed, that the Commission is the bulwark of the public utility corporations, that it is of no value to the people, is the anxiety of the corporations to make the Commission a permanent body, the existence of which would be guaranteed by the Constitution.

Mr. Willcox, who cannot be accused of being

unfriendly to the entrenched powers generally and public utility corporations particularly, strongly urged before the Constitutional Convention of 1915 that the Commission be made a constitutional body; its term to be 10 years.

Honest regulationists are now convinced that regulation as a permanent policy is a failure, others have been compelled to "see" it. Experience is the best teacher; and the costly experience of regulation has taught the people its futility.

Spurred by the failure of their opponents and superbly confident in the soundness of their principle, the collectivists are forging ahead. Their adherents are becoming more and more numerous. The movement is irresistible.

The regulationists realize their diminishing strength and have started a policy of compromise. They have taken for themselves the present and frankly assign the future to the collectivists. They have confessed the impotence of their scheme.

All franchises granted, all contracts entered into between the city and the railway companies bear testimony to these compromises. The 1913 contracts are extremely bulky, covering the relations between the parties in great detail. But this is the very thing the theory of regulation is supposed to avoid. It was intended to do away with rigid agreements.

Throughout the contract runs the confession of the inevitability of public ownership. There is the acknowledgment that the future belongs to the collectivists. The great bulk of the contract is taken up with various details insuring the interest of the corporations in case the people get impatient and demand the subways before 1965. The possibility of such a demand was considered imminent, *not later than ten years after the beginning of operations.* The recapture provisions, though made impotent by the various conditions smuggled into the contracts by the corporations are, nevertheless, indications to what extent the pressure of public opinion compelled the corporation controlled public officials to bow to the collectivists.

Private ownership of public utilities having failed, the policy of regulation having failed, public ownership and operation being inevitable, what kind of public ownership shall it be?

CHAPTER XIII

MUNICIPAL OWNERSHIP WE DO NOT WANT

All roads seem to lead to public ownership.

It is only a matter of time when ownership and operation of public utilities by the government will be considered as commonplace as government ownership of the post-office, the schools, the fire departments, the parks, the bridges, the streets and the water supply, is looked upon to-day.

Besides the Socialist party, which in its larger program includes municipal ownership, one of the old parties, the Democratic party, in this city and state is committed to municipal ownership.

"Specifically," says the Democratic city platform for 1917, "we are in favor of public ownership and operation of all public utilities, including tractions, gas, electricity and the telephone." Mr. Hylan, Democratic candidate for Mayor, laid great stress on this plank in his campaign.

In 1918, when Tammany again assumed control of the city, Senator Wagner, minority leader in the upper house in Albany, introduced a municipal ownership bill giving the cities power, among other things, to build or acquire by purchase or condemnation their transportation facilities and operate them directly, if they chose. The bill was killed in committee.

In the 1918 elections the Democrats won the governorship, but failed to increase their strength in the Legislature to any appreciable extent.

In addition to the flood of municipal ownership bills introduced in the 1919 Legislature by members of all parties, Senator Foley and Assemblyman Donohue, minority leaders of the Senate and Assembly respectively, introduced two enabling acts, which are in principle the same as those sponsored by their party the year previous.

One of the bills, Assembly Bill Int. No. 1102, 1919, short and to the point, ends by saying: "When such determination shall have been so made and approved it shall be unnecessary, anything in this act to the contrary notwithstanding, to obtain the approval, consent or authority of any other body or board pursuant to the provisions of any law, general or special."

This is meant for the benefit of the Public Service Commission. Tammany, considering itself the destined ruler of the City of New York, resents interference by the Commission, a state body, and usually Republican into the bargain.

Many Republicans, though frankly opposed to municipal ownership, are seriously desirous of passing such bills. They are of the opinion that the passage of the bills would only embarrass the Tammany administration. They do not believe their opponents are prepared to go through with the municipal ownership program. They hold, and there is color to such view, that the real reason for Tammany's insistence on municipal ownership is the opposition to it by the Republicans. Since the political game demands an "issue," Tammany is quite willing to make municipal ownership "the issue."

This seems to be true, because in cases where the city administration did have the power and the opportunity to redeem its campaign promises it failed to do so. The Tammany-public-ownership worthies at the mere sight of a chance to enact a public ownership ordinance drew their heads into their private-ownership, corporations-ridden shells.

"On February 28, the Socialist Aldermanic delegation, through Aldermen Vladeck, Held and Wolff, introduced an ordinance providing for the operation by the City of New York of passenger and other car service over the Williamsburgh Bridge.

"When the Socialists introduced their ordinance the company was operating under a permit which was to expire on March 31, 1918—this permit has since been extended six months—when, it was expected, a new contractual arrangement would be entered into between the company and the city.

"The ordinance was intended to prevent this by municipalizing the line. . . .

"It was pointed out by the Socialists that the company had been realizing a net annual profit of approximately 100 per cent. on an original capitalization in 1904, when it was organized, of $100,000. Its net corporate income for the fiscal year ending June 30, 1917, according to the company's own balance sheet, was $92,742.24.

"The Socialists further pointed out that the bridge, the tracks on the bridge, the wiring and terminals, were—and are—the property of the city.

"Here was—and still is—an opportunity for

the administration elected on a municipal ownership platform to prove its sincerity."*

The ordinance was emphatically voted down. The Bridge Operating Company received another extension.

This action casts serious suspicion on the sincerity of the Democrats. In the light of these facts, their loud demands for "permission" from the Republican Legislature to enact municipal ownership is almost as impressive as the frantic demands of "Let me go!" made on a friend by a man drawn into a fight, who, at heart, is too cowardly to go through with it, but must put up an appearance and "make a showing."

When a party in power, with no commendable past in its favor, refuses to put into practice definite campaign promises—and what it still pretends to strive for where it is prohibited by law—upon an occasion such as was presented to it by the expiration of the Bridge Company contract, an occasion most favorable to the city, it is well to be on guard before endorsing its kind of municipal ownership.

Perhaps the desire of certain railroad corpora-

* The Socialists in the Board of Aldermen, by E. Clark and C. Solomon, pp. 16, 17.

tions to get rid of some old, dilapidated and unprofitable lines, or some such consideration, would move the city administration to live up to its campaign promises. Such practices would be neither new nor striking.

When Mr. Gaynor, who (for a Tammany candidate) was exceptionally intelligent and sincere, ran for Mayor, in 1909, his classic speeches were largely able exposés of the 1900 and 1902 subway steals, and solemn promises to save the city from similar transactions.

"And now," said Mr. Gaynor, in a speech delivered in Tammany Hall, on October 19, 1909, "if I may get away from my notes, I will say just a few words in regard to some of the important issues of the campaign. My friends, we are going to build subways, for the city is going to build subways. *We do not intend that a single subway franchise for it shall be passed over to those men* who erected your street railways over here to have bonds and stocks sold out to the community on the highest figures, and then the road thrown into bankruptcy, the same as your roads are over here to-night, and have been for three years, not a dividend paid on them meanwhile.

"Oh, you men of Manhattan! I fear you do not always know what is occurring right among you—the most scandalous chapter in the history of New York, and it has evoked very little public indignation. The men that did it are said to be good men. They hold their heads high. . . .

"Nobody ever put a dollar into the building of the present subways except the city; nevertheless, the day it was opened and you met to celebrate the opening of it, how many people in the city of New York stopped to think that, although they had put every dollar into it, they did not own it when it was completed, but that those who got into it have it for 75 years, before it comes back to the City of New York.

"*I can tell you that during the next four years we will build the subways for the city and none of those people will so much as get their little finger into it.*"

This is a fair sample of the kind of campaign speeches and promises made by candidate Gaynor. No doubt this issue as much as any other was responsible for his election.

The people had a right to expect public ownership of the contemplated subways. They had a right to expect that the subways would be built "for the city."

What actually happened has already been told. "Those people" not only got "their little finger into it," but their whole hand. In spite of his pledges and promises, in spite of the tremendous "public indignation" it has evoked, the same Mayor Gaynor entered into the 1913 contracts, which not only surrendered the subways that were to be built but have amplified and guaranteed the robberies of the first and second contracts which he so eloquently attacked.

If the public ownership of Hylan is to be no better than that of his, in many respects, much worthier predecessor, the people will be thankful to him if he leaves matters as they are.

It often happens that sincere advocates of certain reforms most actively oppose these reforms when introduced with a view of strengthening the very interests they are designed to combat. The German Social-Democrats, champions of social ownership of the means of life, were the strongest opponents of certain government monopolies. They opposed Bismarck when he sought to create a tobacco monopoly. They opposed Kaunitz in his wheat monopoly project. They opposed the transformation of the Reichsbank into a government bank. The opposition was based squarely on the ground that it would strengthen the arm of the ruling class, the junker and capitalist elements, and would furnish them with facilities for more intense spoliation.

The Socialists in this city, the foremost advocates of public ownership, may be faced with the unpleasant task of opposing public ownership *à la Tammany*.

Several questions will have to be carefully examined before public ownership, proposed by the believers in the established order, is indorsed by the working class generally and the Socialists in particular.

1. Will the city take over only those lines it deems necessary? Or will it acquire all lines, taking the fat along with the lean? Or will it take the lean and leave the fat to the corporations?

2. If the city takes over the entire system, will it lease some lines to operating companies and operate others directly, or will it operate all lines as a unit, as one system?

3. Upon what basis does the city expect to acquire these lines?

4. How will the workers employed on the city-owned lines be protected? Will they be in no better circumstances than other city employees?

The questions under the first head are important because the city will need to raise a gigantic sum of money for which no preparation is being made by those in authority. If the entire transportation system is not acquired, support of public ownership will depend, among other things, on the particular lines the administration seeks to acquire. Even if the city is to take over the entire transportation system care must be taken that this move is not used as a cloak to relieve the companies of many useless and profitless lines. There are some lines that cannot be properly placed in a local transportation system.

The second question is of moment because every bill now pending in the Legislature giving the cities power to acquire public utilities expressly empowers them to lease these properties. If the sponsors of the bills really mean to embark upon a policy of public ownership, and extend it to all fields where private ownership proves unbeneficial, they would not seek a right to do that which has so shamefully been employed for the past 20 years as a means of robbing the city. The subways in New York are "leased" to the Interborough and the B. R. T. The people had enough of "leases."

The kind of public ownership that would have for its purpose the mere changing of lessors instead of abolishing them altogether should not receive the support of true advocates of public ownership. Here, again, the motives and future plans of the old party public-ownership politicians must be studied.

For many reasons the third question is the most complex. Constitutional property rights, the science of finance, the honesty of the appraisers, the interference of the courts, the shrewdness of the corporations, the breadth of vision and public faithfulness of the administration are some of the essential elements involved.

Excepting the provisions in the various bills giving power to the cities to acquire the properties by "purchase and condemnation," the proponents of government ownership have not clearly indicated upon what financial basis they will acquire the roads.

Senator Newlands, speaking before the joint

committees on Interstate and Foreign Commerce of the Congress of the United States, November 20, 1916, gave an intimation of the plan in view for acquiring privately owned railroads by the government.

"The plan of acquiring national ownership," said Senator Newlands, "would not be difficult. It would not involve the entire readjustment of the present system. It would be easy to authorize the Interstate Commerce Commission to institute suit and *condemn the shares of stock of railroads* in the country engaged in interstate commerce, *leaving the bonds outstanding as a lien upon the property.* Thus the interests of the stockholders would be purchased by the nation and the Interstate Commerce Commission could step into the position of director of the various corporations, with their present organization of officials and employees, and could gradually work out a method of national administration."

Thus, the acquiring of property by condemnation under the present complex relations of corporate industry is nothing more than the condemnation of worthless stock, the assumption of obligations to pay interests on, and redeem, when due, the entire outstanding bonded indebtedness.

It should be borne in mind that the railroad properties in this city are mortgaged several times their worth. No matter how little the government may pay for the stock, and even if it be acquired without cost, the government would still be nothing more than the collecting agent for the capitalists. It would collect the mighty tribute capital has levied upon the people. It is doubtful whether high finance, unless it refrains for political reasons, will not become the staunchest supporter of this kind of government ownership. The bankers would much rather have the government as their debtor than private companies.

In stepping into the shoes of the private companies, the Government, as debtor, would have to pay a high interest and heavy bonus to which the bankrupt corporations bound themselves in their worst days of financial helplessness. The Government would also have to pay interest on, and redeem, the bonds issued against "dead capital," and such other debts.

Although government ownership under these conditions would eliminate millions of dollars paid in dividends, still, it is doubtful whether the responsibilities of guaranteeing bad debts, badly incurred, running into hundreds of millions of dollars, is worth the gain. Looking at it from a class point of view, the capitalist class would gladly give up dividends, consider them as a sort of premium, paid annually to the Government, for insuring its actual and alleged bonded investments.

Such seems to be the government ownership about to be inaugurated by those who believe in the preservation of the present system.

Three questions must here be answered:

1. Will this kind of government ownership be an improvement, financially, upon present conditions? Not to any appreciable extent.

2. Will such kind of government ownership be conducive to the movement seeking to transform society "by degrees" from capitalism to Socialism? Indeed not.

3. Can advocates of public ownership, with a view of extending its principle to other socially necessary industries leading to the elimination of the capitalist system, support such government ownership? Hardly.

The assumption by the Government, in December, 1917, of the great railroad system of the country with its 260,000 miles of railways, its

1,000,600 employees, and its investment of $17,-500,000,000, might have proven the greatest argument in favor of permanent public ownership of railroads and its extension to other public utilities if not for the financial losses suffered by the Government in spite of the decided raise in rates. The public is not aware, of course, that these losses are largely due to the high tribute paid to the private owners under the contract.

A concrete case like this serves as an excellent weapon in the hands of reactionaries who readily take advantage of the balance sheet to prove the "failure" of public ownership, and particularly public operation.

For the genuine supporters of the public ownership idea to try to explain this failure is good labor lost. Public ownership must prove successful if it is to serve as an example to those who want "to be shown." If it has not this value, then private ownership should be preferred until such time as the real thing—not the millennium but just real public ownership—can be introduced.

Thousands of working men and women will not support public ownership until the fourth question is answered, and answered properly.

The experience of workers in the employ of the government is most disappointing. Rights they enjoy in private employ are denied them when they are similarly employed by the government. The Federal employees are forbidden to exercise their fundamental rights as citizens. They are forbidden to engage in political activities, a right which private employers would not dare to take away openly. They are generally denied the right to organize, and when permitted that, they are strictly forbidden to strike.

In the government employ, as we have it now, the worker is paralyzed. His weapons are taken away. His only means of redressing his grievances is the petition. This he refuses. He has acquired enough self-respect to know not to crawl and beg when he can demand and get.

Thus far, who is less free than the government employee? Against the government it is almost impossible to struggle, much less to win.

With the private employer the workers have a better opportunity to win. His comparatively limited economic resources, fear of bankruptcy, and a desire not to get "in bad" with the public often make him concede to the workers' demands. If the industry is well organized both contestants have an even chance. The great mass of people, conveniently designated as "the public," is a neutral party and, of late, is even inclined to favor the cause of labor.

Such is not the case when the workers face the government. On strike, they are branded as traitors. They are confronted by the unconquerable economic strength, as well as the formidably organized physical and moral power of the government.

The open shop, in government industry, is reinforced with the open jail.

The workers remember the street cleaners' strike in this city several years ago, and the attitude assumed by the municipality at that time. Nor do they forget the action of the Government in the truck-drivers' struggle against a private employer who happened to carry United States mail, a federal government industry.

In these struggles, the state assumed the attitude of defender of organized society. It asserted its authority as a police-state when, as a matter of fact, the workers were striking not against the police-state, the state, defender of public peace and order, but against the state as employer of labor, the state as teacher, streetcleaner, highway builder, mail carrier and railroad owner.

Labor will hesitate to support a public ownership which does not guarantee it the right to organize in its own defense, and strike, if necessary, against the employer—state.

Thus, from every point of view, it will be seen that public ownership *per se* is not necessarily even a partial victory for the collectivists' program. The establishment of a state industrial feudalism may so paralyze the forces of labor, so weaken it in its struggle, that its ultimate emancipation will be postponed rather than hastened.

Only a public ownership that will strengthen the arm of labor in its struggle for economic freedom, that will facilitate the transformation of society from capitalism to Socialism, that will weaken the authoritarian state and strengthen the industrial functions of the state is worthy of the support of Socialists in particular and labor generally.

Public ownership is so imminent, there is so much demand for it from all quarters, that it is important to outline briefly the general principles of a public ownership that should be demanded and, nothing short of it accepted.

If we are to be spared a period of popular lethargy towards the collectivists' demands likely to result from the disappointment of an over-expectant people in public ownership, at least these three elements indispensable to a sound program of municipal ownership should be insisted on.

1. A sound policy of public finance. This is a troublesome question. Different groups in society advocate different policies, depending largely upon their economic interests.

2. The establishment of a scientific administrative organization. Inefficiency, lack of economy and corruption have been the stock arguments against public ownership.

3. The rights of those employed in the municipal or state-owned industry must not only not be curtailed but liberally extended.

Each of these three elements will be discussed in turn.

CHAPTER XIV

PUBLIC OWNERSHIP AND FINANCE

As a prerequisite to acquiring the surface, elevated and subway lines, the municipality should appoint a commission of engineering experts, who should be removed, as far as possible, from the influences of the traction trust, to study the entire transit problem. Taking all matters into consideration, the commission should determine which lines are essential to an efficient, unified and sufficient system of transportation for the people of Greater New York.

Thereupon a Board of Appraisers should determine the actual present physical value of the lines, rolling stock and equipment. But no single item should be estimated under any circumstances to be worth above original cost.

Franchises should not be valued at more than what the city actually received for them. If the city received no compensation there should be none paid to the company, regardless of how much the present owners allege to have paid for them to the party to whom the franchises were originally granted.

Real estate owned by railroad corporations, by reason of the growth of the community, has in most cases risen in value entirely out of proportion to the original cost. To the extent that these properties are necessary to the transit system they should be appraised; but their value shall not exceed cost.

All leases, contracts and agreements should be cut right through, until the original owners are reached. All red tape and complicated dealings must vanish, simplicity should take its place.

No fear need be entertained regarding the disintegration of the existing "systems." There are no systems now. Only when all necessary lines come under unified control can system be instituted in place of the chaos and anarchy that now prevail.

Working within the framework of present society with its established legal relations and constitutional guarantees, the city will have to indemnify the owners for the roads. The basis for such payment shall be the value established by a Board of Appraisers. To raise money for that purpose the city should issue municipal bonds. As matters stand to-day, they will be bought largely by the financiers.

During the life of the bonds, the holders will be entitled to draw interest in the tens of millions of dollars annually. This annual tribute to be paid to the possessors of the money bags mirrors the absurdity of a system under which a community is taxed to the extent of tens of millions of dollars annually, by a small group of people who have absolutely nothing to do with the productive, directive, or in any other constructive way with the industry.

It is estimated there are $1,000,000,000 worth of bonds outstanding against the properties of the local transportation system in Greater New York. Judging by the few companies of which some sort of physical valuations were taken, over half of these outstanding bonds are not represented by property.

Evens Clark, director of the Socialist Aldermanic Research Bureau, prepared a table of figures from Reports of the Public Service Commission and the Tax Commsision for 1918, showing the outstanding securities of the railroad companies upon which the public is expected to pay interest and dividends and the values of the properties upon which the corporations pay taxes. The following is an extract from that table:

NAMES OF COMPANIES	Securities Outstanding	Value of Property Reported to Tax Commissioner
Hudson & Manhattan R. R. Co.	$122,360,183	$21,898,000
N. Y. Consolidated R. R. Co....	102,550,000	38,501,539
Second Avenue Line..........	10,722,000	3,596,761
New York Railways System...	95,838,889	57,511,301
Third Avenue System..........	70,333,961	25,935,223
Brooklyn Rapid Transit System	66,620,962	45,047,792

These figures are self-explanatory.

Of the various lessons to be drawn from these figures this stands out, namely, that the value of the properties are far less than the outstanding securities indicate. The probable present physical value of the roads in Greater New York, determined on the basis laid down for the appraisers, would be less than $500,000,000.

Assuming the interest paid on the bonds now outstanding to be only 5 per cent., and assuming the municipality will pay as high a rate on its bonds it will still save over $25,000,000 annually. Added to this the millions paid every year in guaranteed dividends and in rentals, the city would save from $50,000,000 to $75,000,000 annually.

There are methods of obviating the private bankers entirely. Other countries have paved the way. Belgium solved its problem of finance for municipal enterprises by organizing the "Credit

Communal," an inter-municipal bank. Belgium learned by experience how not to pay millions of dollars in interest to private bankers. It found the collective credit of the municipality, properly organized, to be just as good and better than the private banks.

"In order to facilitate for the municipalities the loans that they are often obliged to negotiate at the time of undertaking any work of local utility," says E. Vendervelde, "the Government, at the suggestion of a Socialist, Haeck, encouraged the establishment of the 'Credit Communal,' a corporation having no other stockholders than municipalities; . . ."*

Scarcely had this bank been established when its organizers were authorized to found another bank, the General Savings Annuity Bank. These banks are highly successful.

With all the hundreds of millions of dollars going through private banks, annually, in the carrying on of municipal business in New York State, an inter-municipal bank would be a most powerful financial institution.

A corporation, organized under the laws of

*** Socialism vs. the State, E. Vandervelde, p. 151.**

New York, with municipalities as the sole stockholders, the inter-municipal bank would soon become a clearing-house for all municipal financial transactions. Branches could be conveniently established in different cities. The purpose of this bank would not be to charge large underwriting fees, nor to hold business up for usurious interests, nor to manipulate the financial market for private profit, but rather to become a social instrument to facilitate social effort.

The taking over of the entire transit system would no doubt be the greatest single enterprise yet undertaken. To leave the finances of a business involving hundreds of millions of dollars to the city administration to be handled in the same manner as the other municipal finances are handled, is deliberate business suicide. Even if the city were not in the hands of Tammany with its notorious appetite for things glittering, there would still be objection to confusing the finances of the Municipal-Governor with those of the Municipal-Transporter. There must be financial autonomy for the railroad business. The budget of the Industrial-Government must be completely divorced from the budget of the Police-Government.

Rules of strict accounting should be maintained. The necessary funds for repair, deterioration, re placement of properties, redemption of bonds, as well as a general reserve fund for all sorts of emergencies, should be established.

Bonds issued for the purpose of raising money to pay for the roads or for building extensions and new lines, must be amortized. Under the present arrangement the fare-payers must cover all the expenses, including the amortization of the bonds, which is another way of making them pay for the first cost of construction.

This seems to be unjust and unsound. It is sufficient if the fare is large enough to cover the maintenance of the roads at top-notch efficiency, the cost of operation, and the maintenance of a reserve and replacement fund.

The owners of real estate in undeveloped or partly developed sections of the city, as well as those owning property in the business heart of the city, should pay all or part of the cost of first construction, in as much as the benefit derived from a proper system of transportation accrues to them in the form of increased real estate values.

Subways, such as the city has built and is now

in the process of building, extending as they do beyond congested centers, add very greatly to the value of real estate in those districts which have not been built up prior to the construction of these subways because of lack of transit facilities. It is a matter of common knowledge that the real estate values in Washington Heights, The Bronx and in the business section of the lower part of Broadway, due to the building of the subways, have risen enormously. Rent profiteering in The Bronx particularly reached scandalous proportions.

Shall the real estate interests be permitted to enjoy exclusive financial benefits from the community-built rapid transit? Shall the fare-payers be taxed at both ends of the pole? Shall they pay for the construction of transportation lines and also pay higher rents because of having constructed these lines? Clearly, this is not just.

A commission should be appointed to make a careful and scientific study of the areas and extent to which real estate values have risen by reason of the construction of transportation lines.

The "unearned increment" thus ascertained, should be assessed to the full amount, and the money used for an amortization fund to retire all bonds issued by the municipality for the purpose of purchasing the traction system. If these assessments are in excess of the funds needed for amortization, the residuum may be used to build extension routes and new lines in sparsely-populated sections in order to develop this metropolis to its full possibilities, and relieve its congested neighborhood in which people are herded like cattle. The principle of assessing the rise in real estate values due to public improvements should be applied to all extensions and new lines built.

If, however, these assessments do not yield sufficient to cover the amortization of the first cost of construction, or the bonds issued for the purpose of acquiring the transportation system, the farepayers should supply the difference.

Another way of obtaining the same results is by issuing assessment bonds against each piece of property for the full amount of the "unearned increment," which would not be a lien upon the city, but upon the property assessed. The only objection to this method is the comparative difficulty the marketing of these bonds would present. With an inter-municipal bank this difficulty would be obviated.

The principle of assessment bonds is already

in operation covering local improvements. The cost for street openings, pavements, sewers and such other expenses is defrayed by assessing the property in the vicinity benefiting therefrom.

There has been a tendency of late to establish public ownership for fiscal reasons. When the State, monarchical or republican, by reason of its general extravagances and huge military and naval appropriations swells the budget beyond a point where, what is called legitimate taxation, does not suffice to finance it, it embarks upon a policy of government ownership of certain recognized monopolistic industries for what it can get out of it.

With the tremendous war loans and the interests they bear there will be a strong temptation on the part of our own government to go into public ownership and use the profits for the purpose of relieving the taxpayers. In municipalizing the traction system in this city care must be taken, therefore, that the fiscal considerations for governmental purposes shall play no part at all in the arrangement. The principle of public ownership is social service, convenience and safety to the public, and decent, human treatment and proper pay to those employed in the system.

Under public ownership fares would be reduced instead of raised.

A derivative table of figures for 1918, prepared by Mr. Clark from data in the Reports of the Public Service Commission, show, among other things, the actual cost of carrying passengers on New York local lines and also the profits made upon each passenger:

NAMES OF COMPANIES	Average Cost to carry Passengers in Cents	Average Profit Made on Each Passenger in Cents
Interborough Rap. Tr. System..	2.6	2.4
New York Railways System....	3.8	1.2
Third Ave. System............	3.8	1.2
Brooklyn Rapid Transit System.	3.7	1.3
N. Y. Consolidated R. R. Co....	2.8	2.2
Hudson & Manhattan R. R. Co.	3.7	3.3

These figures are highly illuminating in view of the persistent demand for higher fares.

The outstanding fact is that with all the waste, high salaries and bonuses to officials, the known figures prove that the fares could be considerably reduced.

Under a unified system of operation and control the principle of one-city-one-fare could be realized.

Autonomy of finance in government industries, the divorce of the Industrial-Government from the Police-Government has as its indispensable compliment autonomy of administration.

Chapter XV

PUBLIC OWNERSHIP AND ADMINISTRATION

Along with the promise on the part of the leading railroad companies that they will go bankrupt, a promise they at this writing have redeemed, there was instituted a powerful and incessant propaganda against public operation of the roads.

The principal arguments used against the municipalization of the traction systems were these: The government is incompetent. It cannot be relied upon to do practical work. Political corruption, political favoritism, political interference in the management of this gigantic industry will result in inefficiency and lack of economy. The service will be demoralized.

However true these arguments are, the companies are least qualified to make them. Their testimony cannot be taken at face value because they are interested witnesses. It is they and members of their tribe who corrupted public officials by bribing them in order to get franchises. They duped administrations to surrender to them the city's traction system. They have financed and supported the parties in power. They have bitterly opposed those who sought to effect a change either in the form or substance of the present government. They have clamored for the imprisonment of those who wished to purify the government and purge it of its vices. They, therefore, are not fit to hold up the government of their own creation to ridicule and contempt.

Municipalizing the traction systems does not necessarily mean politicianizing them. Undoubtedly, if the roads are to be municipalized there must be complete separation between the political administration of the city and the administration of its railroads. It would be disastrous indeed if the political ward-healers were to have power to temporize with this industry.

The present method of extending government functions is by erecting additional departments, which become a part of the political state, subject to all the political influences and shortcomings characteristic of our government. This must be guarded against in the public ownership of railroads. Although all precedent is in favor of the department, results at home and the experience of other countries argue against it. A distinction must be made between the extension of a government function political in its nature and one that is industrial.

It would be deplorable indeed if the department method of administration were pursued. Should the Department need locomotives, or rails, or coal, or anything else, it would have a resolution introduced in the Board of Aldermen. Some diligent members of the majority happen to be absent. The minorities desirous of settling ever-present grievances against the party in power would take advantage of the situation to block the ordinance. While the Aldermen were playing politics, trying to find out whether the contract is to be made "with public letting" or "without public letting," the business would be hampered.

Department administration opens the door to Tammany Hall, or for that matter, to any other political organization happening to be in control. A department is usually the servant of the majority party instead of the city as a whole. Formally, orders to the administrators of the department are given by the elected officials, actually the orders are framed by the political boss. The election district captains and the district leaders who need patronage to insure success at the polls would multiply the present political corruption if they had a department in charge of a half a billion dollar business at their disposal. They could play havoc with their opponents.

A corporation should be organized, an organization of a special kind, clothed by law with civil personality, and act in its own name as owner of the transit system. The corporations should be governed by a board of directors consisting of representatives of the city elected by the Board of Aldermen and the employees of the lines.

Of the directors representing the city each recognized political party in the Board of Aldermen should be entitled to representation proportional to the vote cast for that party at the last regular election. In that way a true cross-section of the people's will can be secured on the Board of Directors. Such an arrangement will also remove from the administration of the industry the absolute rule of the majority so brutally and disastrously employed in the administration of the political affairs of the city.

The employees must be represented on the Board of Directors for their own protection and for the best interests of the roads. Representation on the board will bring the working force into direct contact with the shaping of the policies of the industry.

The general legal features of a private corporation would characterize this public corporation, except, of course, there would be no stock, no dividends, no profits and no selfish interests to be served. The corporate method should be borrowed from capitalism because it secures autonomy, the only guarantee of success in public ownership.

The corporation should have power to name the management. Responsibility must be decentralized. Efficiency and economy depend upon the avoidance of rigid bureaucratic rule.

"In the administrative, like the political order," says E. Vandervelde, a Socialist theoretician and a practical man, "the characteristic of the present system is centralization pushed to the extreme.

"From top to bottom, in almost any administration a system of management reigns looking much more to decision than to execution, paralyzing initiative and suppressing responsibility. In the Belgian State railways, for example—and as much might be said for other countries—an engineer in charge of a shop cannot modify in any way the processes of the system of operation in the service which is directly entrusted to him without the authorization of his chief, who in his turn has to ask the authorization of the management, which again, in most cases, has to ask the approval of the council of administration.

"In short, every initiative has to pierce three zones in which it has much chance of meeting obstacles in routine ignorance or hostility. If it starts from a man of much will power, it will overcome these obstacles, but as men of this type form the exception the initiative quickly finds itself rebuffed, and oftener than not it ends by becoming null."*

Those who have been employed by one of the state or city departments and have been victimized by its red tape and bureaucratic management will appreciate the picture drawn by Vandervelde.

Private ownership, at the pain of extinction, has learned to decentralize the management of industry. General decisions are made on top while the initiative for particular application of

---

* Collectivism and Industrial Evolution, E. Vandepelde, p. 131.

these decisions are left to those who are entrusted with the actual work. Individual initiative and responsibility go together.

As authoritarian a state as Prussia of the Kaiser had learned to give its industries administrative autonomy. It could get results in no other way.

A French engineer, M. Weiss, hostile to government ownership of coal mines, has this to say about the government-owned mining industry of Sarre:

"Considered as a whole, the Administration of Mines is endowed with a strong organization, which permits it to compete in the industrial field with the best managed private enterprises. We must say that in spite of the habits of authority inherent in the race, in spite of what may be called Prussian militarisms, *the administration is highly decentralized; responsibilities are well defined; a large initiative is left to the agents who carry out orders. . .* The working force is well disciplined and profoundly attached to the mine. It is through this solid organization that the Prussian State, operating the largest mine field in the world has arrived at *brilliant results*, in spite of the difficulties in all State operation."*

The phenomenal success of the Swiss railway system is ascribed by the students of the question chiefly to its complete administration autonomy as regards the Central Government which owns it.

Although the members of the directing board are appointed by the Federal Council, the Federal Assembly and the different Cantons—all of which are government bodies—the divorce of the administrative functions of the railroad system from the functions of the government as such, is so complete as to remove all political influence and bureaucratic red tape from the successful management of the roads.

Municipal ownership of the transit system in New York will be successful only when we, profiting by the experience of other countries and borrowing the good features of private ownership, will establish complete financial and administrative independence of the roads.

---

* Quoted in Socialism vs. the State. E. Vandervelde, pp. 168-169.

CHAPTER XVI

PUBLIC OWNERSHIP AND THE WORKERS

One of the most perplexing problems the proponents of public ownership must solve before labor will embrace their program is the establishment of proper relations between the working force and the government.

The old conception of a government employee is incompatible with his modern status. When the State was little else than a policeman its employees were functionaries. They were agents of the sovereign power. In fact, while in office they were the soverign power.

To have permitted these functionaries to organize into a union would have been equivalent to permitting them to conspire against the public powers, against the State. If the organization had been effective it would have meant the setting up of private interests against the general interest. It was, therefore, perfectly logical to forbid public officials to organize.

But workers employed in government-owned industries are not public officials. They are not functionaries. There is a vast distinction between the government as policeman, as soverign, and the government as transporter, as employer, as business manager.

The corollary of financial and administrative independence and their freedom from government interference is the independence of the working force and its freedom from the tyranny of rigid bureaucratic rule.

The workers in a municipally-owned traction system would be helpless if each individual were left to himself to settle his grievances with the management. His chance of securing a respectful hearing would be remote indeed. Experience amply teaches that.

The workers should be guaranteed the right to organize and strike, if necessary. They should be permitted to affiliate themselves with the rest of organized labor in order to augment their strength and to compare well with the almost inexhaustible economic strength of the employer-state.

Under private ownership, although the workers are accorded the legal right to organize and strike, their "right" is often of no great value to them because of the gigantic and powerful corporations they must fight. A mere right to organize and strike under municipal ownership is not sufficient, for the municipality being even more powerful than any single private corporation could certainly reduce that "right" to nothing by assuming a stubborn and hostile attitude to its working force. A deliberate policy must be established of dealing with the workers collectively. Working-class organization should be part of the organization of the business proper.

Collective bargaining is now recognized as an effective deterrent of strikes. Machinery should be set up to settle disputes as they arise. The instrument should include representatives of the working force, the management and a person chosen by both sides.

It is to be presumed that along with a director of equipment, a director of supplies, a director of construction, etc., there would also be a director of labor. This director of labor, or whatever name the person in charge of labor be called, should be elected by the workers and ratified by the board of directors. An agent of the workers, by their own unmolested choice, the director of labor would enjoy their confidence. Being ratified by the board of directors, he would become the link between the workers and the board. By means of this link, differences may be adjusted without resorting to either arbitration or strike.

As mentioned in the previous chapter, the workers in their organized capacity should be represented on the board of directors by persons of their selection. This would devolve responsibilities upon the workers. Conscious that the decisions spring partly from their direct representatives, partly from their indirect representatives—for they are part of the community at large whom the Board of Aldermen represents, the workers would strive to execute those decisions with a will and a purpose that would insure successful service.

The demand for democracy in industry is growing more audible from day to day. If that be true of privately owned industry, how much more true is it of industries publicly owned?

The suggestions here outlined are a mere beginning. With time the entire management of industry should be in the hands of labor.

Chapter XVII

PUBLIC OWNERSHIP AND SOCIALISM

Public ownership is not Socialism. Even if most industries were owned by the municipality, state and nation, it would still not be Socialism; it would be State capitalism.

Socialism is predicated on three propositions.

1. The nature of the State must change. It must cease to be a power of coercion and of domination. It must become an organ of management of industry, of the coordination of human affairs. It must be constructive.

2. There must be established a system of collective ownership and democratic management of *all* socially necessary means of production and exchange.

3. All income derived from ownership must be abolished. Only by one's labor, muscular or intellectual, shall one earn his livelihood.

To-day the primary purpose of the State is domination; its secondary functions are the economic affairs of the people.

Under Socialism the primary purpose of the State will be the management of the economic affairs of the people; its secondary function will be political.

The more functions of an industrial nature the State assumes, the more it enfeebles its authoritarianism.

The change in the nature of the State may come by degrees, peacefully, legally, or it may come by violence. Socialists desire a peaceful transformation, and they frankly say so. As to whether such will be the process depends more upon the powers that be than upon the Socialists.

If political liberties are infringed upon, freedom of speech, press and assemblage denied, political corruption at the polls permitted and even protected; if Black-Hundred organizations formed to hound economic heretics are encouraged and even subsidized; if workers are deported and sent to jail for their views, there may develop among labor a feeling of mistrust, a lack of faith in the entire legal machinery as an instrument of progressive social change and ultimate emancipation.

Working class tactics are generally determined by those who make the rules under which the workers find themselves rather than by their own desire.

Public ownership of what is now generally understood as public utilities is not sufficient, the Socialists claim. Modern industry has become social in its nature, and what is social in its nature should be socially owned. To leave such industries to private individuals is a menace. And events have proved the truths of this.

Socialists do not propose that the miners own the miners, the factory employees own the factories, or the railway workers own the railways. They believe in collective ownership.

It may be put this way: Generally, if the industry is municipal-wide its ownership would reside in the municipality; if it is state-wide the state would own it; and if it is of a national character, the nation would own it.

The management of these industries, however, should be in the working force. The workers should elect their foremen, managers, superintendents, etc. They should have democracy in industry.

In discussing "Public Ownership and Finance," it appeared that under the present system of legal property rights and relations, even if the municipality acquired the traction lines, it would have to pay to the capitalists an annual tribute of about $30,000,000 to $40,000,000 in the form of interest. If Socialism merely meant the extension of this method to other industries, the capitalists would lose little, for the Government would collect a large tribute from the people and deliver it periodically to a parasitic class. Of course, that is absurd.

Once society decides that the capitalist class is useless in the scheme of things, that capitalism is an anachronism, it will by the same force and power sweep aside all former property rights and relations, and will establish a code in harmony with the new social conditions.

Under Socialism, income from legal possesion will be abolished. Unless a person is incapacitated either physically or mentally, he will have to work, to become useful.

No parasitism under Socialism.

UNIVERSITY OF MICHIGAN
3 9015 02093 0122

www.ingramcontent.com/pod-product-compliance
Lightning Source LLC
LaVergne TN
LVHW011203110826
845150LV00006B/1302

* 9 7 8 1 4 2 5 5 1 8 8 4 4 *